CW00322106

THE OFFICIAL

Arsenal

MISCELLANY

THE OFFICIAL

Arsenal

MISCELLANY

DAN BRENNAN

CONSULTANT EDITOR FRED OLLIER

hamlyn

To my mum, Peggy, and to Rebecca for making the last year such a special one.

First published in Great Britain in 2004 by
Hamlyn, a division of Octopus Publishing Group Ltd
2–4 Heron Quays, London E14 4JP

This updated edition published in 2005

ISBN-13: 978-0-600-61434-0
ISBN-10: 0-600-61434-4

A CIP catalogue record for this book is available from the British Library

Printed and bound in the UK

10 9 8 7 6 5 4 3 2

Every reasonable effort has been made to acknowledge the
ownership of copyright material included in this book. Any errors
that have inadvertently occurred will be corrected in subsequent
editions provided notification is sent to the publisher.

All statistics correct up to the end of the 2004/05 season.

FOREWORD

In 1946, a group of local boys were kicking a football on Avenell Road. When the ball ran under a car parked outside the Arsenal Stadium entrance, the smallest of them, an 11-year-old lad, was dispatched to retrieve it. As he crawled under the vehicle, he heard a booming voice behind him enquire, 'What are you doing there, boy?' It belonged to none other than George Allison, the Arsenal manager at that time. He told the boy to report back to him the following day. Not daring to question him, the youngster did as instructed, and was subsequently employed as a runner, carrying messages between the office and the commissionaires on the main entrance ... and over half a century on, I am still working at the Club.

I can honestly say that I still experience the same excitement and pride working for Arsenal today as I did all those years ago. This is a club with an impressive pedigree: over the years, we have seen the League title brought triumphantly to Highbury on 13 occasions (I hope 2004/05 will see the fourteenth), the FA Cup has been Arsenal's nine times and I have witnessed three Doubles, two European triumphs and the last-minute drama of that momentous night at Anfield in 1989.

But it's not all been about the football. I have also seen Arsenal stadium play host to a world title fight between Cassius Clay and Henry Cooper, and the Highbury pitch transformed into an ad hoc emergency landing pad for an air rescue helicopter!

The Official Arsenal Miscellany is a celebration of a unique Club, which has always been proud of its past and its traditions, while seeking to remain at the vanguard of progress and innovation. Hence when we redesigned the Club's badge in 2002, it was done under the enduring ethos of 'Tradition with Vision' – a spirit that has been alive since the Club's first days in 1886, through the golden era of Herbert Chapman in the 1930s, to the recent feats of Arsène Wenger's team of international stars.

This book is not an exhaustive collection of statistics, nor is it an attempt to tell the history of the Club from A to Z. The past and present of a football club is about much more than the sum of its results and its silverware, never more so than in the case of Arsenal. It is a rich tapestry comprised of personalities, traditions, and defining moments, on and off the pitch. ▶

The last 118 years have thrown up a wealth of fascinating incidents and stories. Did you know, for example, that Arsenal once beat a French national XI 26–1, or that in the 1950s, Highbury regularly staged charity matches between teams of boxers and jockeys? Were you aware that the former Icelandic Finance Minister was once an inside forward for the Gunners, or that there are teams in Czechoslovakia and Portugal that have based their colours on Arsenal's strip?

If *The Official Arsenal Miscellany* succeeds in achieving its goal, then even the most seasoned and fanatical of Arsenal supporters will, during a random excursion through the pages that follow, find something to surprise and intrigue them.

We hope you enjoy it.

Ken Friar, Director, Arsenal Football Club, 2004

ARSENAL TRADITIONS (1)

Long sleeves or short?

Since the days of Herbert Chapman, tradition at Arsenal has dictated that all players must wear the same length of shirt sleeves for any given match. The decision on whether the sleeves are long or short always rests with the captain. In 2003/04, skipper Patrick Vieira tended to opt for long sleeves, while if Ray Parlour was deputising the sleeves were likely to be short.

ARSENAL 26 FRANCE 1

It might sound preposterous, but a century ago, on 5 December 1904, that was the score when Arsenal entertained a Parisian XI which was, by general consensus, actually the French national team. The game took place nearly six months after FIFA had been founded in Paris.

The scorers for Arsenal were: Watson 7, Hunter 5, Coleman 4, Briercliffe 4, Buchan 2, Linward 2, Blackman and Ransom.

In 1910, Arsenal narrowly avoided being taken over by Fulham, and indeed might have gone out of business altogether. On 19 May, tucked away in the Sports Intelligence section of *The Times*, in between the croquet and cricket scores, and a report on a certain Mr Diggle's billiard match, came the following notice:

WOOLWICH ARSENAL CLUB

A sub committee appointed by the Football League with representatives of Woolwich Arsenal and Fulham Football Clubs at the Imperial Hotel, London, met yesterday, when the question of the future of Woolwich Arsenal Football Club was discussed. The sub-committee declined to sanction the proposal that the Fulham Club should take over the Arsenal Club, but agreed to the formation of a new board of directors, consisting of Mr G.H. Leavey (Chairman of the former board of directors), Mr Norris, Mr Allen and Mr Hall (of the Fulham Club).

The new directors will appeal for subscriptions for shares, but failing adequate support from the local public, they will themselves subscribe sufficient money to justify them in going to allotment; and they will continue the Woolwich Club for one year at least. If in that time the local public show by their support that they are desirous of retaining First Division football in the district, the Club will be continued, but if not it will then be the duty of the directorate to consider what is best in their own interests, and in the interests of the shareholders.

In the end, Sir Henry Norris, together with William Hall, assumed a 37.5 per cent stake of the new share capital – Norris went on to take control of the Club, and three years later took it north of the river. According to one version of events, for two months in 1910, a certain Tottenham Hotspur featured on the shareholders register with 100 share holding*.

* The Real Arsenal Story, *Alan Roper (see bibliography)*

HITTING THE BAR

Some pubs within ten minutes of Arsenal Stadium:

The Gunners, Blackstock Road
The Arsenal Tavern, Blackstock Road
The Auld Triangle, Plimsoll Road
The Bank of Friendship, Blackstock Road
The Compton Arms, Compton Terrace
The Highbury Barn, Highbury Grove
The Drayton Arms, Drayton Road
The Woodbine, Blackstock Road
The Junction, Corsica Street

SPANISH PUZZLE

A Spanish newspaper headline on 27 October 1952 screamed:

ARSENAL PLAYER MURDERED DURING A MATCH. SCOTLAND YARD INVESTIGATES!

The piece beneath it read:

An English footballer of the Arsenal has been killed during a football match played at Highbury. Scotland Yard has opened an inquiry. The players who took part in the match have been questioned, as well as the referee, who would appear to be the murderer.

The story bore an uncanny similarity to the plot of *The Arsenal Stadium Mystery*, which had been published, and then turned into a movie, before World War Two. This was more than just coincidence.

It turned out that the French newspaper *L'Equipe* had recently bought the serialisation rights to the story and was publicising it all around Paris. Someone sent the French publicity to a Spanish editorial office, and they mistook fiction for fact.

See also: The Arsenal Stadium Mystery (page 124)

£8 IN WINTER, £6 IN SUMMER

In days gone by, standard practice at Arsenal, as elsewhere, was to pay players a slightly reduced rate over the summer during the close-season. Alf Fields, who joined the Club in 1936, remembers that the top whack was '£8 a week in the winter and £6 a week in the summer, with 10 bob (50p) expenses.'

Fields recalls the yearly visit to the manager's office, when the players found out whether they had a contract for next season: 'I can remember one lad going in to find out about his contract and he comes out of the manager's office and says: "I've got eight and six."

'The next lad goes in and the manager offers him seven and five. So he says: "But you gave the other player eight and six." So the manager replies: "Yes, but he's a better player than you." To which the fellow answers: "Maybe so – but not in the summer!"'

THE THINGS THEY SAY (1)

'It's one—nil to the Arsenal.
That's the way we like it.'

Manager George Allison to his team, in The Arsenal Stadium Mystery.

See also: The Arsenal Stadium Mystery (page 124)

DERBY DAZZLER (1)

RAY KENNEDY
3 May 1971 • Spurs 0 Arsenal 1
First Division, White Hart Lane

The goal that seals the title in 1970/71, and part one of that season's League and FA Cup Double. With minutes to go, John Radford's header is blocked by Pat Jennings, then keeping goal for Spurs. George Armstrong plays the ball back in and this time Kennedy is there to head in off the underside of the bar. A draw would have been enough, but Kennedy's goal provides the icing on the cake.

CHAMPION GUNNERS (1)

Division One 1930/31

	P		Home					Away				
		W	D	L	F	A	W	D	L	F	A	Pt
Arsenal	**42**	**14**	**5**	**2**	**67**	**27**	**14**	**5**	**2**	**60**	**32**	**66**
Aston Villa	42	17	3	1	86	34	8	6	7	42	44	59
Sheffield Wed	42	14	3	4	65	32	8	5	8	37	43	52
Portsmouth	42	11	7	3	46	26	7	6	8	38	41	49
Huddersfield T	42	10	8	3	45	27	8	4	9	36	38	48
Derby County	42	12	6	3	56	31	6	4	11	38	48	46
Middlesbrough	42	13	5	3	57	28	6	3	12	41	62	46
Manchester City	42	13	2	6	41	29	5	8	8	34	41	46
Liverpool	42	11	6	4	48	28	4	6	11	38	57	42
Blackburn R	42	14	3	4	54	28	3	5	13	29	56	42
Sunderland	42	12	4	5	61	38	4	5	12	28	47	41
Chelsea	42	13	4	4	42	19	2	6	13	22	48	40
Grimsby Town	42	13	2	6	55	31	4	3	14	27	56	39
Bolton W	42	12	6	3	45	26	3	3	15	23	55	39
Sheffield Utd	42	10	7	4	49	31	4	3	14	29	53	38
Leicester City	42	12	4	5	50	38	4	2	15	30	57	38
Newcastle Utd	42	9	2	10	41	45	6	4	11	37	42	36
West Ham Utd	42	11	3	7	56	44	3	5	13	23	50	36
Birmingham	42	11	3	7	37	28	2	7	12	18	42	36
Blackpool	42	8	7	6	41	44	3	3	15	30	81	32
Leeds Utd	42	10	3	8	49	31	2	4	15	19	50	31
Manchester Utd	42	6	6	9	30	37	1	2	18	23	78	22

ABOUT A BOY

In a career terminated by knee problems and deafness, Cliff 'Boy' Bastin held Arsenal's scoring record for half a century. His 178-goal tally, amassed over 17½ seasons at the Club, was only eclipsed – by Ian Wright – in 1997. His achievement was all the more remarkable as he was mostly a winger.

Bastin's arrival at Arsenal happened almost by chance. In May 1929, manager Herbert Chapman went to check out a Watford player. But his ▷

attention was instantly diverted by a hugely talented 17-year-old outside left who was playing for the Hornets' opponents, Exeter City. The next day, Chapman travelled to Devon and bought Bastin for £2,000, which was an unprecedented fee for a teenager in those days.

Bastin's looks were so boyish that when he reported for training, the commissionaire thought he was a schoolboy and refused to let him in.

After two seasons at the Club, the 19-year-old Bastin had earned League Championship and FA Cup winners' medals. He was also the original Arsenal 'Iceman'. 'He had a trait few of us are blessed with: an ice-cold nerve,' observed Tom Whittaker, then the Gunners' trainer. Bastin died in his native Devon in 1991, aged 79.

———— OTHER SPORTING EVENTS AT HIGHBURY ————

1916–1919
Baseball matches for US servicemen in Great Britain

10 October 1921
International rugby match: England v Australia For the Lord Mayor of London Fund for Relief of Famine in Russia

12 August 1949
Cricket match: Denis Compton's Benefit: Arsenal v Middlesex County Cricket Club

11 August 1952
Cricket match: Jack Young's Benefit (floodlit): Arsenal v Middlesex County Cricket Club

9 August 1955
Cricket match: Leslie Compton's Benefit: Arsenal v Middlesex County Cricket Club

25 October 1955
Ladies' international hockey match (floodlit): England v USA

21 May 1966
World heavyweight boxing match: Cassius Clay v Henry Cooper

See also: Cooper v Ali (page 41)

ALAN SUNDERLAND'S NEIGHBOURS

Former Arsenal striker Alan Sunderland – scorer of the famous last-gasp winner in the 3–2 FA Cup Final victory over Manchester United in 1979 – until recently lived on the Maltese Island of Gozo . . . just down the road from the comedian Billy Connolly, who owns a holiday home there.

While playing for Arsenal, Sunderland also boasted a famous neighbour – Spurs' Argentinian midfielder, Ricky Villa.

1930 FA CUP FINAL

26 April 1930 • Wembley • Attendance: 92,486
Arsenal 2 Huddersfield 0 (Goals: James, Lambert)
Formation: 2-3-5

PREEDY

PARKER   HAPGOOD

BAKER   SEDDON   JOHN

HULME   JACK   LAMBERT   JAMES   BASTIN

FROM FORWARD LINE TO FRONT BENCH

Few footballers can have enjoyed careers quite so remarkable as Albert Gudmundsson. The Icelandic striker joined the Club in 1946, becoming only the second Arsenal player from outside the United Kingdom and Ireland.

Denied a work permit that would have enabled him to sign professional terms, he played only a handful of games before moving on to AC Milan, and later Nancy, Nice and Racing Club de Paris, eventually becoming Iceland's first ever professional player.

Later he did return as a guest player for Arsenal's tour to Brazil in 1951. Alf Fields, who was at Arsenal during Gudmundsson's time at the Club, later recalled him as 'an exceptionally good player, and a very suave, sophisticated-looking character.'

On hanging up his boots after he had returned to play in Iceland, in 1957 Gudmundsson became a successful businessman. He was later named president of the Icelandic Football Federation, and was instrumental in organising a match between Arsenal and Iceland's national team in 1969.

In the 1970s he entered politics, being elected first mayor of Reykjavik and later a member of parliament. When his party was voted into office, he served in Iceland's government, first as Industry Minister and then as Finance Minister. Later, a political dispute prompted him to form his own party, which won about ten per cent of the vote. Eventually he became a diplomat, serving as Iceland's ambassador to France and Spain.

Gudmundsson's son, Ingi Albertsson, recalled: 'Being associated with such a great club as Arsenal helped my father's career in many ways. He maintained his ties with the Club, and never forgot his time there. My father died on 7 April 1994.'

ALEX JAMES TAKES A CRUISE

In November 1935, George Allison felt that inside left Alex James was jaded and decided to send him on a cruise. James was, according to his team-mate Eddie Hapgood, 'the world's worst sailor', so he was not too pleased at the idea, but Allison was not a man to be argued with.

When the Scot got to St Katherine's Dock, his sense of dismay was increased. Having packed all his fanciest clothes, he discovered that the vessel in question was not a cruise liner but a cargo vessel, carrying a load of sheepskins to Bordeaux.

'I'm not going on that!' James apparently told trainer Tom Whittaker, who had come to see him off. 'Boss's orders,' Whittaker replied. So off he sailed.

See also: Like son, like father (page 75)

NUMBER CRUNCHING (1)

708,401: the total number of Arsenal Corinthian figurines sold in the UK between March 2002 and March 2004.

ALF KIRCHEN'S LUCKY STRIKE

Alf Kirchen, Arsenal's dynamic outside right of the 1930s, was famous for his ability to shoot powerfully from long range. One particular Kirchen rocket, in a wartime match against Brentford, failed to find the target, but proved a blessing for one football fan. The shot was heading straight for the face of a defender, who raised his arms to protect himself and conceded a free-kick for handball. Denis Compton netted direct from the kick to score the game's only goal.

Some time later, Kirchen and Compton received letters thanking them for the result, each with a £10 note enclosed. Later still, during World War Two, when Kirchen had been forced to retire from football through injury and been invalided out of the RAF, he received another letter from the same person, this time with a cheque for £25 enclosed.

It transpired that the sender had selected Arsenal, on his football pools coupon, to beat Brentford that day, and had won what was in those days a small fortune of £4,000. Had Arsenal not recorded a victory he would have won nothing.

DERBY DAZZLER (2)

LIAM BRADY
23 December 1978 • Spurs 0 Arsenal 5
First Division, White Hart Lane

The most incredible goal of an incredible derby. A young Liam Brady wins the ball in the Spurs half before advancing a few yards to the edge of the box and unleashing a physics-defying left-foot curler of Roberto Carlos proportions that bends into the top right-hand corner of the net.

ALL-STAR XI

Between 2002 and 2004, 52 former Arsenal players from different eras were asked to name their best ever Gunners team. Patrick Vieira featured in a remarkable 45 line-ups, with Tony Adams, Liam Brady and Thierry Henry not far behind. Based on the most votes cast, the 'team of teams' slots neatly into a 4-4-2 formation, lining up as follows:

Goalkeeper	**Pat Jennings**	(28 votes)
Right back	**Lee Dixon**	(19)
Central defender	**Frank McLintock**	(25)
Central defender	**Tony Adams**	(43)
Left back	**Kenny Sansom**	(29)
Right midfielder	**George Armstrong**	(29)
Central midfielder	**Patrick Vieira**	(45)
Central midfielder	**Liam Brady**	(42)
Left midfielder	**Robert Pires**	(24)
Forward	**Thierry Henry**	(42)
Forward	**Ian Wright**	(22)

Subs: **Dennis Bergkamp** (13), **David O'Leary** (13), **Pat Rice** (13), **Bob McNab** (12), **David Seaman** (11)

CHAPMAN INNOVATIONS (1)

A tube by any other name

Herbert Chapman was not simply an outstanding football tactician and organiser, he also had a subtle understanding of how to market his product.

Arsenal's move north of the Thames in 1913 had been prompted primarily by a need to draw in more support. Through his lobbying of the local authorities to re-christen Gillespie Road tube station as Arsenal, Chapman ensured that the Club was placed even more firmly at the centre of the capital's sporting map.

The renaming took months of negotiation and required a huge logistical effort – millions of tickets had to be reprinted, signs and maps replaced and machinery reconfigured. Arsenal remain the only football team in London with a tube station named after them.

WHEN DENNIS MET IAN

Two of the greatest Arsenal strikers of all time, Ian Wright and Dennis Bergkamp, formed a breathtaking partnership on the pitch. But their first encounter took place entirely by chance . . . in a petrol station on the M25. Dennis Bergkamp tells the story:

'I'd come over from Holland to spend a few days here and have my medical before signing. We were on the M25 and stopped at a petrol station to fill up. I pulled into a space behind another car, but just then the car in front pulled out. I stayed put. The car behind me had to go round me to get to the pump in front. I could see the driver; he didn't look happy and was saying: "What are you doing?"

Then he got out of his car. It was Ian Wright! When he realised it was me, he was like: "Look, it's Dennis! Come on, come on – it's Dennis." Then he just started hugging me. He'd just heard on the radio that I'd signed for Arsenal. We'd never met before. It really was the biggest coincidence I've ever known. It was amazing that I met the person who was going to be my playing partner for the next few years like that.'

ALL THE PRIZES

Division One/Premiership Champions (13 times):
1930/31, 1932/33, 1933/34, 1934/35, 1937/38, 1947/48, 1952/53, 1970/71, 1988/89, 1990/91, 1997/98, 2001/02, 2003/04

Division One/Premiership runners-up (seven times):
1925/26, 1931/32, 1972/73, 1998/99, 1999/2000, 2000/01, 2002/03

FA Cup winners (ten times):
1930, 1936, 1950, 1971, 1979, 1993, 1998, 2002, 2003, 2005

FA Cup finalists (seven times):
1927, 1932, 1952, 1972, 1978, 1980, 2001

League Cup winners (twice):
1987, 1993

League Cup finalists (three times):
1968, 1969, 1988

European Fairs Cup winners (once):
1970

UEFA Cup finalists (once):
2000

European Cup Winners' Cup winners (once):
1994

European Cup Winners' Cup finalists (twice):
1980, 1995

National Premier League Ladies Champions (seven times):
1992/93, 1994/95, 1996/97, 2000/01, 2001/02, 2003/04, 2004/05

Women's FA Cup winners (six times):
1993, 1995, 1998, 1999, 2001, 2004

Women's League Cup winners (eight times):
1992, 1993, 1994, 1998, 1999, 2000, 2001, 2005

FA Youth Cup winners (six times):
1966, 1971, 1988, 1994, 2000, 2001

FA Premier Youth League Champions (once):
1997/98

FA Premier Academy League Under-17 Champions (once):
1999/2000

FA Premier Academy League Under-19 Champions (once):
2001/02

FA Premier Academy League Under-19 runners-up (once):
1999/2000

ARSENAL ON SIX CONTINENTS

As well as players from the length and breadth of Europe, Arsenal have also featured footballers from Africa, Asia, Australasia, and North and South America. That means that the Gunners have fielded players from every continent except Antarctica!

- Asia: **Junichi Inamoto**
- Africa: **Danny Le Roux, Kanu, Christopher Wreh, Jehad Muntasser, Kolo Toure, Lauren**
- Australasia: **John Kosmina**
- North America: **Danny Karbasyoon, Frankie Simek**
- South America: **Edu, Gilberto, Silvinho, Juan, Paulinho, Nelson Vivas, Fabian Caballero**

AND FOR MY FIRST (HAT-) TRICK

Just two players have scored hat-tricks on their full league debuts for Arsenal – Ian Wright and Jermaine Pennant – both, coincidentally, against Southampton.

Ian Wright ....28 Sep 1991 ......Southampton 0 Arsenal 4
Jermaine Pennant ...7 May 2003 ....Arsenal 6 Southampton 1

Just to rub it in, Wright also scored a hat-trick in the 1991/92 return fixture against the Saints, which Arsenal won 5–1.

Pennant's treble formed one half of another record. He and Robert Pires, who grabbed the other three goals that evening at Highbury, became the first Premiership players ever to score hat-tricks for the same side in the same match.

BULL'S-EYE BONANZA

In 1902, a cash-strapped Woolwich Arsenal, languishing in the Second Division, came up with a curious idea for boosting the Club's coffers: an archery tournament on Plumstead Common. Similar events had been organised by clubs in the north, but this was the first time a club in the south of England had undertaken such an enterprise.

It proved a huge success, and raised a net sum of £1,200 from participation fees and ticket sales. The funds were used to bolster the squad with several new signings, including Tommy Shanks, a future Ireland international and penalty specialist, Jimmy Bellamy.

ANIMAL MAGIC

Some animalistic Arsenal nicknames:

Frank Hill . . . . .Tiger

David O'Leary . . . . .Spider (for his spidery reach when making interceptions)

Luis Boa Morte . . .The Boa Constrictor, Spider Man

Vladimir Petrovic The Pigeon (his Yugoslav nickname was Pizhon, gained for his ability to 'flutter' round the pitch)

Patrick Vieira . . . . .Giraffe Legs, Paddy Long Legs

Oleg Luzhny . . . . . .The Moose/The Horse (known as 'The Moose' in Ukraine, he was in fact dubbed 'The Horse' in England thanks to a mistranslation)

Gilles Grimandi . . .The Wonder Goat

David Platt . . . . .Plattypuss

Christopher Wreh Stingray

Kanu . . . .*Papillo* (that's Latin for 'butterfly'). Kanu owns a Football team in Nigeria, which he has called Papillo FC

Joe Hulme . . . . .The Eel (*L'Anguille* – French for eel – was the name given to the winger by the Paris press during a match against Racing Club in 1930)

Percy Sands . . . . . . .The Tame Elephant. The Arsenal captain in their first years at Highbury was so called because he was so good natured off the pitch and such a tough competitor on it

See also: AKA (page 112)

ARSENAL PLAYERS' NAMES
IN CHINESE CHARACTERS

In 2004, a version of the *Official Arsenal Magazine* was published in Hong Kong. This is how the players' names look to Chinese readers:

列文 Jens Lehmann

基拔圖施華 Gilberto

羅倫 Lauren

皮裏斯 Robert Pires

高路托利 Kolo Toure

柏金 Dennis Bergkamp

蘇甘保 Sol Campbell

亨利 Thierry Henry

艾殊利高爾 Ashley Cole

雷恩斯 José Antonio Reyes

龍格保 Fredrik Ljungberg

ARSENAL DOCS

Four medical men – an Englishman, a Scot, an Irishman and a Welshman – have played for Arsenal.

Dr James Paterson (outside left, 1920–24 and 1925–26):
A Londoner, Paterson qualified as a doctor in Scotland. He won the Military Cross for his work as a medical officer, serving in the London Scottish Regiment during World War One. He set up practice as a GP in Clapton and quit the game in 1924, but was lured out of retirement for a final season by Herbert Chapman in 1925. Paterson played 70 League games for Arsenal.

Dr James Marshall (inside forward, 1934–35):
A Scot, who was already a full international by the time he joined Arsenal from Rangers for £4,000, which was no small sum in those days. Marshall, who later worked as a medical officer for Bermondsey Council, played four League games for Arsenal.

Dr Kevin O'Flanagan (winger, 1945–49):
O'Flanagan joined the Club at the end of World War Two after taking a job at a hospital in Middlesex. He was an all-rounder who also excelled at rugby and athletics, and represented Ireland at both. Later he became doctor to the Irish Olympic team and served on the Sports Medical Council. He played 14 League games and two in the FA Cup for Arsenal.

Dr Leigh Richmond 'Dick' Roose (goalkeeper, 1911–12):

A doctor in bacteriology who maintained his amateur status throughout his football career, Roose was a Welsh International who played for several top clubs. He played 13 League games for Arsenal.

See also: Doctor Roose's lucky shirt (page 46)

CHAMPION GUNNERS (2)

Division One 1932/33

	P	W	D	L	F	A	W	D	L	F	A	Pt
				Home					Away			
Arsenal	42	14	3	4	70	27	11	5	5	48	34	58
Aston Villa	42	16	2	3	60	29	7	6	8	32	38	54
Sheffield Wed	42	15	5	1	46	20	6	4	11	34	48	51
WBA	42	16	1	4	50	23	4	8	9	33	47	49
Newcastle Utd	42	15	2	4	44	24	7	3	11	27	39	49
Huddersfield T	42	11	6	4	32	17	7	5	9	34	36	47
Derby County	42	11	8	2	49	25	4	6	11	27	44	44
Leeds Utd	42	10	6	5	39	24	5	8	8	20	38	44
Portsmouth	42	14	3	4	39	22	4	4	13	35	54	43
Sheffield Utd	42	14	3	4	50	30	3	6	12	24	50	43
Everton	42	13	6	2	54	24	3	3	15	27	50	41
Sunderland	42	8	7	6	33	31	7	3	11	30	49	40
Birmingham	42	13	3	5	40	23	1	8	12	17	34	39
Liverpool	42	10	6	5	53	33	4	5	12	26	51	39
Blackburn R	42	11	6	4	48	41	3	4	14	28	61	38
Manchester City	42	12	3	6	47	30	4	2	15	21	41	37
Middlesbrough	42	8	5	8	35	33	6	4	11	28	40	37
Chelsea	42	9	4	8	38	29	5	3	13	25	44	35
Leicester City	42	9	9	3	43	25	2	4	15	32	64	35
Wolves	42	10	4	7	56	48	3	5	13	24	48	35
Bolton W	42	10	7	4	49	33	2	2	17	29	59	33
Blackpool	42	11	2	8	44	35	3	3	15	25	50	33

SIGN HERE

Since 1932, Arsenal have kept a guest book for noteworthy visitors to Highbury. The entries range from foreign secretaries and royals to former world heavyweight boxers and pop musicians. Here is a selection:

1933 ....**Harold Lloyd** (American star of the silent screen)
17 Nov 1934 ......**Lady Edward Spencer-Churchill**
(wife of Winston Churchill's great-uncle, Lord Edward Spencer-Churchill)
29 Dec 1934 ......**Stanley Rous** (chairman of the Football Association)
5 Oct 1935 ....**Bud Flanagan and Chesney Allen**
(members of The Crazy Gang)
23 Jan 1937 ......**Anna Neagle** (actress)
3 May 1947 ......**Ernest Bevin** (Labour Foreign Secretary)
26 Mar 1949 .....**Montgomery of Alamein** (military commander)
2 Feb 1950 ....**King Faisal of Iraq**
16 Nov 1957 .....**Anthony Crosland**
(Labour MP and future Foreign Secretary)
12 Jan 1984 ......**Joe Frazier** (Ex-world heavyweight boxing champion)
1988 ....**Phil Collins** (musician)
4 Apr 1991 ....**John Major** (Conservative Prime Minister)
1 Feb 1992 ....**John McCarthy** (journalist and former Beirut hostage)
26 Dec 1994 .....**Douglas Hurd** (Conservative Foreign Secretary)
30 Dec 1995 .....**Rod Stewart** (musician)
21 Apr 1997 ......**Sir Richard Attenborough** (film director)
21 Apr 1997 ......**Michael Howard** (Conservative Home Secretary)
21 Apr 1997 ......**Anne Widdecombe** (Conservative MP)
March 2000 .....**Robbie Williams** (musician)
March 2000 .....**Rinchinnyamin Amarjargal**
(Prime Minister of Mongolia)
November 2001 ..**Bertie Aherne** (Irish Premier)
2002 ....**George W Bush** (US President) and family
8 Nov 2003 ....**Han Zheng** (Mayor of Shanghai)
18 Dec 2003 ......**The Prince of Wales**
6 May 2004.......**Aleksander Kwasniewski** (Prime Minister of Poland)
27 May 2004 .....**Albert Finney** (actor)

Warsaw, 4 May 1998

Mr Peter Hill-Wood
Chairman
Arsenal Football Club
Highbury
London

Dear Mr Hill-Wood,

I congratulate you most heartily on Arsenal's brilliant game and victory over Everton last Sunday, which led to Arsenal securing the Premiership Championship. The style in which Arsenal won the Premiership with two games to spare, after winning the last ten, is most admirable to me and gives me a personal satisfaction.

It is no secret that I have been a great supporter of your club since at least 20 years. I cherish an Arsenal T-shirt that I received from the Foreign Secretary Robin Cook last November. On my last visit to London in March this year I realised that even the British Prime Minister Tony Blair was well aware of my bias towards the Arsenal.

If one asked me what makes me support the Arsenal over so many other splendid English soccer teams, my rational answer would be that it is the quality, potential and ambition of the club as shown by the impressive collection of League Championships, FA Cup and European honours. But I must admit, that your white and red colours, like the colours of the Polish national flag, play on my emotions as well.

My warm congratulations go to the manager Arsène Wenger, the coaching staff with Pat Rice and Boro Primorac, the captain Tony Adams and his team, and all the other 'Gunners'.

I wish you further victories!

Aleksander Kwasniewski

THE THINGS THEY SAY (2)

*'You can have who you want if you can
persuade them to leave Highbury.'*

*Arsenal boss Tom Whittaker's crisp reply when asked by another
manager if he had any players he wanted to sell.*

WOOING THE FRENCH

Much as Thierry Henry, Patrick Vieira and Robert Pires have been hailed
as 'The Three Musketeers' of English football, during the 1930s similar
compliments were flying in the other direction.

During that decade the Gunners' annual trip to France, to play Racing Club
de Paris, ensured celebrity status for Herbert Chapman's team on the
other side of the English Channel, and several players acquired French
nicknames in the sporting press. Cliff Bastin became *Le Feu d'Artifice* (The
Firework), Joe Hulme was *L'Anguille* (The Eel), while Alex James was
dubbed *Le Miracle* (The Miracle).

See also: Racing across the channel (page 88)

NUMBER CRUNCHING (2)

36,000: the approximate number of Arsenal birthday cakes sold in the UK
between December 2001 and December 2003.

HAIL CAESAR

The magnificently named Caesar Augustus Llewelyn Jenkyns, a centre
half, became the first footballer to earn international honours while at
Arsenal when he was capped for Wales in 1896. Having signed from Small
Heath in Birmingham in 1895, he spent just one season at Arsenal, during
which he was Club captain. He moved on in 1896 to Newton Heath (later
Manchester United).

GOOD OLD ARSENAL

Good Old Arsenal was recorded as the Gunners' official song for the FA Cup Final in 1971, with lyrics apparently written by one Jimmy Hill! It reached number 16 in the charts. A revamped version is still used used to welcome Arsenal onto the pitch at Highbury.

> *Good Old Arsenal*
> *We're proud to sing your name*
> *While we sing this song*
> *You'll win the game*

Other gems recorded by the Arsenal squad over the years include:

> **1932** *Here We Go Again*
> **1972** *Arsenal, We're On Your Side*
> **1978** *Roll Out The Red Carpet*
> **1979** *Super Arsenal,* featuring *Liam Brady* on the B-side
> **1989** *We're Back Where We Belong*
> **1993** *Shouting For The Gunners*
> **1998** *Hot Stuff,* with *You'd Better Believe It* on the B-side
> **2000** *Arsenal Number One,* with *Our Goal* on the B-side

LAST OF THE DOUBLE INTERNATIONALS

Arsenal winger Arthur Milton (1945–55) was the last man to become a double international by winning full England caps at both football and cricket. He made six Test appearances for England, while his sole football appearance for his country came against Austria in 1951.

In 1974, when he retired from cricket after notching up 32,000 runs and taking 758 catches, he became a postman in Bristol. When Post Office rules forced him to retire at 60 in 1988, Arthur continued to work his patch, delivering newspapers on his trusty old boneshaker bicycle.

In 2002, when he was awarded an honorary MA by Bristol University, the presentation was made by the Arsenal Director, Ken Friar.

OUR FRIENDS IN THE NORTH

Matches against Glasgow Rangers 1933–1970

In 1933 Arsenal played the first of a long series of friendly matches against Glasgow Rangers that continued into the 1960s. The pair were the outstanding clubs in the United Kingdom during the 1930s, and their regular meetings came to be regarded as Battles of Britain.

The fixture was the joint initiative of Herbert Chapman and his equally pioneering counterpart at Rangers, Bill Struth, who had been in charge at Ibrox since 1920. Given Arsenal's strong historic connection with Glasgow and the surrounding area, which had produced so many of the north Londoners' early players, the encounter had special resonance. The games alternated between London and Glasgow.

After an enforced hiatus during World War Two, the series resumed at Highbury on 17 October 1951. Such was the excitement generated that the match played to a sell-out crowd of 62,012, with a further 10,000 unable to get in.

1933/34................	Rangers 2 Arsenal 0 (Ibrox)
	Arsenal 1 Rangers 3 (Highbury)
1934/35............	Arsenal 1 Rangers 1 (Highbury)
1935/36................	Rangers 2 Arsenal 2 (Ibrox)
1936/37............	Arsenal 2 Rangers 1 (Highbury)
1938/39................	Rangers 1 Arsenal 0 (Ibrox)
1951/52	Arsenal 3 Rangers 2 (Highbury)
1953/54................	Rangers 1 Arsenal 2 (Ibrox)
1954/55	Arsenal 3 Rangers 3 (Highbury)
1955/56................	Rangers 2 Arsenal 0 (Ibrox)
1958/59...........	Arsenal 0 Rangers 3 (Highbury)
1960/61................	Rangers 4 Arsenal 2 (Ibrox)
1962/63	Arsenal 2 Rangers 2
	(Highbury, Jack Kelsey Testimonial)
1966/67	Rangers 2 Arsenal 0 (Ibrox)
1967/68...........	Arsenal 3 Rangers 0 (Highbury)
1968/69...............	Rangers 2 Arsenal 2 (Ibrox)

CHAPMAN INNOVATIONS (2)
From pyramid to W-M

Since the end of the 19th century, most teams had played a 2-3-5 or pyramid formation, often credited as the brainchild of Nottingham Forest's early player Sam Widdowson. With the introduction of the modern offside law in 1925, which reduced the number of defenders that was required to be between attacker and goal from three to two, Herbert Chapman was the first to recognise the inherent defensive inadequacies of the 2-3-5 system.

His new W-M formation – which was so called because the shape of the line-up in a 3-2-2-3 deployment resembled the two letters – galvanised the team into an efficient machine which married tight collective defence with speedy attack.

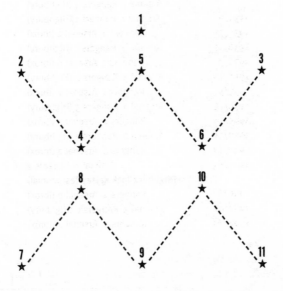

Under the new system, the central midfielder dropped into a centre back position, prompting the two inside forwards to operate in a more withdrawn role. The wide forwards were turned into 'flying columns', encouraged to embark on speedy raids up the flanks.

It is no coincidence that Arsenal's top scorer for half a century, Cliff Bastin, was not a centre forward, but an outside left – a testament not just to the skill of the player, but to Chapman's system.

By the start of World War Two, most English teams had adopted the W-M system, and it remained the most popular formation well into the 1960s.

EUROPEAN CHAMPIONS

Ten Arsenal players have earned a winners' medal in the Champions League (or its precursor, the European Cup) while with other clubs:

- **Brian Kidd** (Manchester United, 1968 v Benfica)
- **Ray Kennedy** (Liverpool, 1977 v Bor. Moenchengladbach, 1978 v Brugge and 1981 v Real Madrid)
- **Tony Woodcock** (Nottingham Forest, 1979 v Malmo)
- **Viv Anderson** (Nottingham Forest, 1979 v Malmo and 1980 v Hamburg)
- **Jimmy Rimmer** (Aston Villa, 1982 v Bayern Munich)
- **Kanu** (Ajax, 1995 v AC Milan)
- **Marc Overmars** (Ajax, 1995 v AC Milan)
- **Davor Suker** (Real Madrid, 1998 v Juventus)
- **Andy Cole** (Manchester United, 1999 v Bayern Munich)
- **Nicolas Anelka** (Real Madrid, 2000 v Valencia)

THE THINGS THEY SAY (3)

'I thought football's greatest honour was representing your country. I was wrong. It was playing for Arsenal today.'

Joe Mercer, Arsenal captain, after the 1952 FA Cup Final against Newcastle United. The Gunners lost 1–0, but put on a heroic display after being reduced to ten men early on through injury.

BEATING THE BLUES

Over a period spanning more than five years, Arsenal built an amazing 17-game unbeaten streak against Chelsea:

31 Jan 1999	**Arsenal 1 Chelsea 0**	Premiership
23 Oct 1999	**Chelsea 2 Arsenal 3**	Premiership
6 May 2000	**Arsenal 2 Chelsea 1**	Premiership
6 Sep 2000	**Chelsea 2 Arsenal 2**	Premiership
13 Jan 2001	**Arsenal 1 Chelsea 1**	Premiership
18 Feb 2001	**Arsenal 3 Chelsea 1**	FA Cup 5th round
8 Sep 2001	**Chelsea 1 Arsenal 1**	Premiership
26 Dec 2001	**Arsenal 2 Chelsea 1**	Premiership
4 May 2002	**Arsenal 2 Chelsea 0**	FA Cup Final
1 Sep 2002	**Chelsea 1 Arsenal 1**	Premiership
1 Jan 2003	**Arsenal 3 Chelsea 2**	Premiership
8 Mar 2003	**Arsenal 2 Chelsea 2**	FA Cup 6th round
25 Mar 2003	**Chelsea 1 Arsenal 3**	FA Cup 6th round replay
18 Oct 2003	**Arsenal 2 Chelsea 1**	Premiership
15 Feb 2004	**Arsenal 2 Chelsea 1**	FA Cup 5th round
21 Feb 2004	**Chelsea 1 Arsenal 2**	Premiership
24 Mar 2004	**Chelsea 1 Arsenal 1**	Champions League QF 1st leg

The sequence was brought to an end on 6 April 2004, in the second leg of the 2003/04 Champions League quarter-final.

BIRDMAN WOOD

Former Arsenal and Scotland goalkeeper George Wood developed a passionate interest in ornithology during his years at Highbury, and is now one of Britain's leading authorities on wading birds.

Having joined the Royal Society for the Protection of Birds, he graduated to the British Trust for Ornithology, where he trained for five years as a bird ringer and has since undertaken a number of scientific surveys. He has spent ten years monitoring populations, movements, and the effects of pesticides on waders in South Lanarkshire.

Wood describes his most exciting experience as ringing a sedge warbler in Douglas Water, then hearing that the bird had been spotted in Gambia.

AN ARSENAL CELEBRITY XI

Over the years, a host of well-known names have featured for the Arsenal Ex-Pro and Celebrity Team, which plays regularly to raise money on behalf of causes supported by the Arsenal Charitable Trust. In real life they are bolstered by the presence of a few seasoned former professionals, but here, just for the sake of it, is a possible all-celebrity XI:

Goalkeeper	**Tommy Walsh**	*Ground Force* gardener
Right back	**Tony Hadley**	Musician (ex-lead singer of Spandau Ballet)
Left back	**Terry Marsh**	Ex-world welterweight boxing champion
Centre back	**Mark Burdis**	Actor (Stewpot in *Grange Hill*)
Centre back	**Frank Thompson**	Sports photographer
Right wing	**Willy Ryan**	Derby-winning jockey
Left wing	**Ralf Little**	Actor (Anthony in *The Royle Family*)
Midfield	**Ronnie O'Sullivan**	Snooker world champion
Midfield	**Mark Ramprakash**	England Test cricketer
Forward	**Leroy Thornhill**	Musician (former member of The Prodigy)
Forward	**Martin Offiah**	Former Rugby League maestro

Willy Ryan, who always wears an Arsenal cannon stitched into his racing colours, is credited (by ex-pro Brian Hornsby) with scoring the goal of the season in 2003/04, a screamer from outside the box.

BRING ON THE BAND

Fans at the game between Arsenal and Manchester City on 22 November 1952 were treated to the following musical numbers by the Metropolitan Police Central Band:

Cleopatra	Mancinelli
The Gondoliers	Sullivan
Victor Herbert Favourites	arr. Lake
Pomone	Waldteufel
Kiss Me Kate	Cole Porter
Playbox	Charrosin
Haymaker's Holiday	Colin Smith
Florrie Forde's Favourites	arr. Stoddon
Champagne Galop	Lumbye

BLINK AND YOU MISSED IT

- Alan Sunderland's strike for Arsenal after a mere 13 seconds in the semi-final second replay against Liverpool in 1980 was the fastest ever FA Cup goal.

- Likewise, Gilberto's goal away to PSV Eindhoven in the Champions League in 2002 – timed at 20.07 seconds – was the fastest ever in the competition. Gilberto's lightning strike beat the previous record – set by Alessandro Del Piero for Juventus against Manchester United in 1997 – by a whole twentieth of a second!

- Another split-second record, of a less distinguished nature, belongs to defender Jason Crowe, who made his debut for Arsenal in the Coca-Cola Cup against Birmingham City on 14 October 1997, coming on for Lee Dixon in extra time. Unfortunately he didn't manage to make it as far as the final whistle, as he was red-carded after precisely 33 seconds on the pitch. Crowe made two more substitute appearances for the Gunners before moving on to Portsmouth.

ARSENAL IN ALBERT SQUARE

Albert Square has always boasted a large contingent of Arsenal supporters. Here is a selection from the *EastEnders* cast, past and present:

Tamzin Outhwaite (Mel Owen)
James Alexandrou (Martin Fowler)
Mark Homer (Tony Hills)
Susan Tully (Michelle Fowler)
Tom Watt (Lofty Holloway)
Michelle Gayle (Hattie Tavernier)
Martin Kemp (Steve Owen)
Joe Swash (Mickey Miller)
Barbara Windsor (Peggy Mitchell)
Gary Beadle (Paul Trueman)
Leonard Fenton (Dr Legg)
Patsy Palmer (Bianca Butcher)
Jessie Wallace (Kat Moon)
Gillian Taylforth (Kathy Beale)

CHAMPION GUNNERS (3)

Division One 1933/34

	P		Home					Away				Pt
		W	D	L	F	A	W	D	L	F	A	
Arsenal	**42**	**15**	**4**	**2**	**45**	**19**	**10**	**5**	**6**	**30**	**28**	**59**
Huddersfield T	42	16	3	2	53	19	7	7	7	37	42	56
Tottenham H	42	14	3	4	51	24	7	4	10	28	32	49
Derby County	42	11	8	2	45	22	6	3	12	23	32	45
Manchester City	42	14	4	3	50	29	3	7	11	15	43	45
Sunderland	42	14	6	1	57	17	2	6	13	24	39	44
WBA	42	12	4	5	49	28	5	6	10	29	42	44
Blackburn R	42	16	5	0	57	21	2	2	17	17	60	43
Leeds Utd	42	13	5	3	52	21	4	3	14	23	45	42
Portsmouth	42	11	5	5	31	21	4	7	10	21	34	42
Sheffield Wed	42	9	5	7	33	24	7	4	10	29	43	41
Stoke City	42	11	5	5	33	19	4	6	11	25	52	41
Aston Villa	42	10	5	6	45	34	4	7	10	33	41	40
Everton	42	9	7	5	38	27	3	9	9	24	36	40
Wolves	42	13	4	4	50	28	1	8	12	24	58	40
Middlesbrough	42	13	3	5	51	27	3	4	14	17	53	39
Leicester City	42	10	6	5	36	26	4	5	12	23	48	39
Liverpool	42	10	6	5	52	37	4	4	13	27	50	38
Chelsea	42	12	3	6	44	24	2	5	14	23	45	36
Birmingham	42	8	6	7	29	20	4	6	11	25	36	36
Newcastle Utd	42	6	11	4	42	29	4	3	14	26	48	34
Sheffield Utd	42	11	5	5	40	25	1	2	18	18	76	31

DERBY DAZZLER (3)

CHARLIE NICHOLAS
21 April 1984 • Arsenal 3 Spurs 2
First Division, Highbury

Champagne Charlie confirms his cult status with a scintillating solo goal, his fourth against Spurs in his maiden season. Picking up the ball outside the Spurs box, he dribbles his way through a crowd of defenders before rounding the keeper and squeezing the ball home from the tightest of angles.

OH BROTHER!

Nine pairs of brothers have been on the books at Arsenal over the years:

The Comptons: Leslie (1931–52) and Denis (1932–50)

Leslie and Denis, who played together against Liverpool in the victorious FA Cup Final team of 1950, were the most legendary of all the Arsenal siblings. Centre half Leslie, who enjoyed a stint as captain, once scored ten goals in a wartime fixture against Clapton Orient. Like his brother, he played cricket for Middlesex. Outside left Denis was, of course, a cricketing hero for England and Middlesex.

The Buists: Robert (1891–94) and George (1896–97)

The Bradshaws: William (1900–04) and Joseph (1901–04)

The Satterthwaites: Charles (1904–10) and Joe (1906–08)

Charles holds the distinction of scoring Arsenal's first ever goal in the First Division, against Wolves on 24 September 1904.

The Neaves: David (1904–12) and Andrew (1908–09)

The Rippons: Willis (1910–11) and Thomas (1911)

The Claptons: Danny (1953–62) and Denis (1957–61)

Born locally, Danny played 233 senior games for Arsenal before later heading Down Under to Australia, while brother Denis came up through the youth ranks and made a handful of appearances for the first team before moving to Northampton Town and then Leyton Orient.

The Gislasons: Valur (1996–98) and Stefan (1996–97)

Two Icelandic brothers who joined the Club at the same time, from two different clubs in their homeland, Fram and Eskifjordur. Valur returned to Fram to become club captain and to represent his country, while Stefan went on to play in Norway.

The Blacks: Tommy (1995–2000) and Michael (1992–1999)

Two players who rose through the youth ranks at Arsenal before moving on to Crystal Palace and Tranmere Rovers respectively. Michael made one appearance in the Champions League against Panathinaikos in 1998.

BOXERS AND JOCKEYS

The annual Boxers and Jockeys football match was a tradition unique to Arsenal, and was a regular part of Highbury's football calendar during the 1950s.

The fixture was the brainchild of Sam Russell, a leading international boxing referee, who suggested a football match between teams of pugilists and equestrians to raise money for the Sportsman's Aid Society. Having put together a team of boxers, he approached two Arsenal players, Jimmy Logie and Arthur Shaw, who were friendly with a number of the day's leading jockeys, many of whom were regulars at Highbury.

The Boxers and Jockeys match on 2 April 1951 was notable for being the first game at Highbury played under floodlights, with the Boxers wearing the red-and-white of Arsenal, and the Jockeys turning out in the colours of Spurs. The Boxers and Jockeys took to the field for the final time at Highbury in 1960, when they joined forces to take on a Showbiz XI.

Sir Henry Cooper, former British and Empire heavyweight champion, who featured for the Boxers a couple of times, and later took centre stage at Highbury for his historic bout with Cassius Clay, has fond memories of the encounters:

> 'It was a really popular event and we used to get decent-sized crowds, at least 15,000 as I recall. You'd have the likes of myself and (fellow heavyweights) Dick Richardson and Brian London, who were all about 6ft 4ins on the one side, and then the jockeys, who were generally a fair bit smaller!
>
> The jockeys used to literally run between our legs, and some of them were right little tricky fellas, who could give as good as they got on the physical side, too. In the end, though, my trainer, Jim Wicks, stopped me playing because the games used to play havoc with my leg muscles!'

See also: Cooper v Ali (page 41) and Boxing clever (page 56)

The programme cover from the 1952 Boxers v Jockeys match. The fixture was a regular feature on the Highbury calendar during the 1950s.

1,900: the approximate number of licensed Arsenal watches sold in the UK between August 2002 and July 2004.

─────────── **1936 FA CUP FINAL** ───────────

25 April 1936 • Wembley • Attendance: 93,384
Arsenal 1 Sheffield United 0 (Goal: Drake)
Formation: 2-3-5 (in practice 3-2-2-3)

WILSON

MALE

HAPGOOD

CRAYSTON

ROBERTS

COPPING

HULME

BOWDEN

DRAKE

JAMES

BASTIN

─────────── **FAREWELL TO THE BUSBY BABES** ───────────

On 1 February 1958, Arsenal played host to Manchester United for a pulsating nine-goal thriller, in front of a crowd of 63,578. Having gone 3–0 down at the break, the Gunners fought back, only to lose 5–4.

The game was made even more memorable for the saddest of reasons. It was the last time United's Busby Babes played on British soil before eight of them lost their lives in the Munich Air Disaster, just five days later.

CHAPMAN INNOVATIONS (3)

White sleeves

Prior to 1933, Arsenal played in all-red tops. During the 1932/33 season, manager Herbert Chapman noticed someone at the ground wearing a red sleeveless pullover over a white shirt, and was struck by the eye-catching effect. His view was that, used on the pitch, it would help his players to pick each other out more easily.

Thus inspired, he came up with a distinctive red-and-white design that has endured ever since. The new kit, which also incorporated the Club's crest, was worn for the first time for a home game against Liverpool on 4 March 1933. Arsenal lost 1–0 on the day, but at the end of the season went on to lift the title once more.

CHAPMAN'S MANAGERIAL SPURS

Legendary Arsenal manager Herbert Chapman took his first step towards management as a result of a chance conversation with a team-mate, Walter Bull.

The two were lying in the bath at White Hart Lane, having played for Spurs in the last match of the 1906/07 season. Bull said that he had just been offered the job of player-manager at Northampton Town (one of Chapman's previous clubs), and suggested to Chapman that he would be better suited to it.

Chapman duly applied and he got the job. Just under two decades later he assumed the helm at Arsenal. The rest, as they say, is history.

NUMBER CRUNCHING (4)

212: the number of hat-tricks* scored by Arsenal players in competitive matches (domestic and European) since 1889, the year the Club first entered the FA Cup.

*Includes one double hat-trick

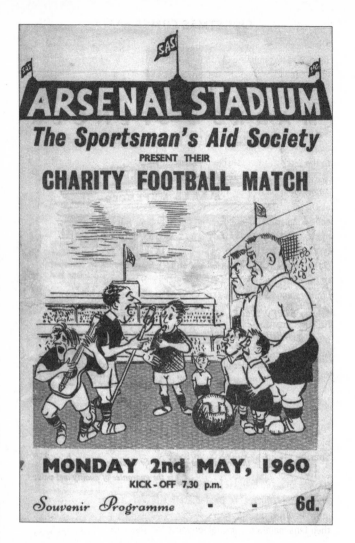

In 1959 and 1960 the annual Boxers and Jockeys charity match took a new twist with the two sets of sportsmen combining to take on a team of 'Entertainers'. Among those who featured for the latter were Tommy Steele and Sean Connery.

CHRISTMAS COMES EARLY

The theatrically named Albert Christmas, who joined Royal Arsenal in 1890, was possibly the Club's first true showman. Soon after starting as a teenager with Wolves, he became a local Black Country favourite because of his breathtaking speed and skill. According to reports of the day, his party piece was to nutmeg an opponent and then do the splits!

Soon this made him a marked man among opponents, and Wolves even employed an ex-boxer to stand in the crowd during matches, and rush on to the pitch at the first sign of aggravation directed at Christmas.

Albert went on to play for Kidderminster Olympic, but when he got a job at Dial Square, he was swiftly recruited by Royal Arsenal, for whom he continued to perform his tricks and quickly established himself as their main scorer.

On one occasion, when asked to turn out for former club Kidderminster in the Weavers Cup Final, he arrived to find the fans greeting him with banners and placards declaring: 'Christmas has come early.'

He continued to work at the munitions factory for many years, and was often to be seen riding about Woolwich on his penny-farthing bicycle. And, apparently, he was still able to do the splits well into his sixties.

CZECH OUT THAT KIT

Founded in 1893, Sparta Prague originally played in black, and then in black-and-white stripes (now their second strip). However, in 1906, Sparta's president, Dr Petrík, visited England and watched Arsenal play.

He was so taken by their red jerseys that he decided to take a set back to Prague, and they were immediately adopted as the Czech club's new strip. Red has been Sparta's colour ever since, and it is the reason that their fans maintain a special fondness for Arsenal.

FREDDIE LJUNGBERG

To tune of *I Love You Baby*

We love you Freddie
'Cos you've got red hair
We love you Freddie
'Cos you're everywhere
We love you Freddie
'Cos you're Arsenal through and through

CHAMPION GUNNERS (4)

Division One 1934/35

	P	W	D	L	F	A	W	D	L	F	A	Pt
				Home					Away			
Arsenal	**42**	**15**	**4**	**2**	**74**	**17**	**8**	**8**	**5**	**41**	**29**	**58**
Sunderland	42	13	4	4	57	24	6	12	3	33	27	54
Sheffield Wed	42	14	7	0	42	17	4	6	11	28	47	49
Manchester City	42	13	5	3	53	25	7	3	11	29	42	48
Grimsby Town	42	13	6	2	49	25	4	5	12	29	35	45
Derby County	42	10	4	7	44	28	8	5	8	37	38	45
Liverpool	42	13	4	4	53	29	6	3	12	32	59	45
Everton	42	14	5	2	64	32	2	7	12	25	56	44
WBA	42	10	8	3	55	33	7	2	12	28	50	44
Stoke City	42	12	5	4	46	20	6	1	14	25	50	42
Preston NE	42	11	5	5	33	22	4	7	10	29	45	42
Chelsea	42	11	5	5	49	32	5	4	12	24	50	41
Aston Villa	42	11	6	4	50	36	3	7	11	24	52	41
Portsmouth	42	10	5	6	41	24	5	5	11	30	48	40
Blackburn R	42	12	5	4	42	23	2	6	13	24	55	39
Huddersfield T	42	11	5	5	52	27	3	5	13	24	44	38
Wolves	42	13	3	5	65	38	2	5	14	23	56	38
Leeds Utd	42	10	6	5	48	35	3	6	12	27	57	38
Birmingham	42	10	3	8	36	36	3	7	11	27	45	36
Middlesbrough	42	8	9	4	38	29	2	5	14	32	61	34
Leicester C	42	9	4	8	39	30	3	5	13	22	56	33
Tottenham H	42	8	8	5	34	31	2	2	17	20	62	30

COOPER V ALI

'The atmosphere was so thick that you could cut it with a knife. Even from the dressing room, all I could hear was the crowd shouting my name.'

Sir Henry Cooper

On 21 May 1966, Arsenal Stadium was the venue for one of the most famous boxing encounters in British boxing history, as Henry Cooper took on Muhammad Ali for the world heavyweight title.

The bout took place in front of a capacity 46,000 crowd, there to see 'the Greatest' and the man who had floored him three years earlier with 'Enery's 'Ammer. Among famous faces ringside were Hollywood legends Lee Marvin, George Raft and Lawrence Harvey. Tens of thousands more fans packed into 17 cinemas to watch a transmission.

The stadium had to be completely reconfigured for the occasion as Ken Friar, Director, recalls:

'The logistics of transforming the ground into a venue suitable for a boxing match were amazing. The whole pitch was renovated and re-seeded before it was boarded over, and we had to make sure there were the necessary gulleys for lighting and TV cable. We then hired hundreds of chairs for the ringside seats.'

Future Arsenal hero Charlie George, then just 16, was among the apprentices drafted in to assemble the ring for the fight:

'It was my first year at the Club. The season had just finished but we all had to position the boards on the pitch in preparation for the fight, and help to build the ring. It wasn't a bad job really – better than cleaning boots or scrubbing the bath for the first team! I think we got paid a few extra shillings for helping out and we got to watch the fight, which was a great experience. Henry was an Arsenal fan and used to come to games. I can remember that the atmosphere was incredible.'

Ali defeated Cooper in the sixth round, but the plucky Englishman cemented his place, and that of Highbury, in British boxing lore.

NORTH LONDON MOVES

When Sol Campbell arrived at Highbury in 2002, he became only the seventh player since World War Two to make the move directly from Spurs to Arsenal. Four players have made the switch in the other direction. Pat Jennings is the only player to travel both ways.

Spurs to Arsenal	Arsenal to Spurs
1949 Freddie Cox	1964 Laurie Brown
1968 Jimmy Robertson	1968 David Jenkins
1977 Pat Jennings	1985 Pat Jennings
1977 Steve Walford	2003 Rohan Ricketts
1977 Kevin Stead	
1977 Willie Young	
2002 Sol Campbell	

See also: Montagues and Capulets (page 114)

See also: Montagues and Capulets (page 114)

OTHER ARSENALS (1)

Arsenal Kiev (Ukraine)
Distance from Highbury: 1,327 miles

CSKA Kiev, originally one of the Soviet Army teams, adopted its new name in January 2002, when the Mayor of Kiev purchased a majority shareholding from the Ukraine's defence ministry.

Since then Arsenal Kiev have been transformed, lifted from perennial mid-table anonymity into a top-five club, challenging regularly for a place in the major European competitions. At one point in 2003, they achieved the previously unthinkable by overtaking mighty city rivals Dynamo in the league table.

ЦЕНТРАЛЬНЫЙ СТАДИОН
„ДИНАМО"

ВТОРНИК **5** ОКТЯБРЯ 1954 г.

МЕЖДУНАРОДНАЯ ВСТРЕЧА

ФУТБОЛ

„АРСЕНАЛ" – „ДИНАМО"

АНГЛИЯ   МОСКВА

Начало в 19 часов

Действителен абонементный талон № 53

Игру судят: Судья международной категории **М. МАЦКО** (Чехословакия)
Судьи на линии · судьи международной категории **Ю. АЛХО** (Финляндия)
                                                      И. КАРАС (Чехословакия)

A year after the death of Stalin in 1953, Arsenal were one of the first English
teams to venture into Soviet Russia, where they lost this encounter with
Dynamo Moscow, played on 5 October 1954, 5–0.

1950 FA CUP FINAL

29 April 1950 • Wembley • Attendance: 100,000
Arsenal 2 Liverpool 0 (Goals: Lewis 2)
Formation: 2-3-5

SWINDIN

SCOTT

BARNES

FORBES

L COMPTON

MERCER

COX

LOGIE

GORING

LEWIS

D COMPTON

WHEN DENNIS PENNIS WORKED FOR SPURS

Arsenal fan and comedian Paul Kaye (aka TV's Dennis Pennis) was once a graphic designer for Spurs. But he couldn't put his loyalties to one side:

'I worked for Spurs in about 1989 or 1990. In fact, I helped design their merchandise catalogue. However, I did expertly integrate a crowd shot on the mag with little AFCs and cannons. They printed 30,000 of them, and I didn't stay there long!'

Kaye is also the man behind the famous 'George Knows' banner which flew regularly at Highbury throughout the 1990/91 championship season.

THE THINGS THEY SAY (4)

'I well remember, as a boy growing up in Hungary, that there was only one club for me – Arsenal.'

Hungary and Real Madrid legend Ferenc Puskas, in Cassell's Sports Quotations.

BILL DICKSON'S INJURIES

Bill Dickson, a half back with Arsenal for just three seasons in the 1950s, suffered what must be one of the most injury-ridden seasons ever in 1954/55. His ill-starred sequence ran as follows:

Dislocated shoulder
Damaged knee ligaments
Appendicitis
Slipped disc

Recurring problems with his shoulder eventually forced him to retire in 1956, and later he became Arsenal's scout in Northern Ireland.

DIVINE INTERVENTION

When Arsenal moved from Plumstead to Highbury in 1913, they acquired the deeds to grounds belonging to St John's College of Divinity, paying £20,000 for a 21-year lease. The land originally comprised two cricket pitches, two football pitches and a dozen tennis courts designed for the use of the divinity students. The deed of transfer was signed by the Archbishop of Canterbury.

Out of respect to their ecclesiastical landlords, Arsenal agreed never to play on Christmas Day or Good Friday. However, in 1925, the Club bought the remainder of the estate, for a total of £47,000. As part of that deal, Club chairman Sir Henry Norris renegotiated the Club's rights to allow them to stage matches over Easter and Christmas.

CHAPMAN'S BUST

The first thing to greet visitors to Arsenal Stadium as they enter the famous Marble Halls is the imposing bronze bust of former manager Herbert Chapman. The bust, commissioned shortly after Chapman's death in 1934, was the work of Sir Jacob Epstein, one of the world's leading expressionist sculptors.

Epstein was born in the USA in 1880 but moved to Paris to study sculpture, before moving to London in 1905 and adopting British citizenship.

DOCTOR ROOSE'S LUCKY SHIRT

Doctor Leigh Richmond Roose, known more simply to Arsenal colleagues and fans as Dick Roose, was, in his day, regarded as one of the finest keepers to play for Wales. He was also something of an eccentric. When the ball was at the other end of the pitch, Roose would often sit leaning against the goalpost and chat to the crowd.

Although a bacteriologist by profession, he had, by all accounts, a casual approach to hygiene. In fact, he refused to wash the shirt he wore under his goalkeeper's jersey, as he considered it a lucky charm. When trainer George Hardy decided to send the shirt off to the laundry, Roose is reported to have flown into a rage.

A RICH SEAM OF TALENT

In the first few decades of the 20th century, a number of players who ended up on Arsenal's books had previously worked in the pits. Here are five ex-miners who played for the Gunners:

Samson Haden: winger 1922–27
Jimmy Brain: centre forward 1923–31
Horace Cope: left back 1926–33
Jack Lambert: centre forward 1926–33
Will Copping: wing half 1934–39

ENGLAND CAPTAINS

Eight Arsenal players have worn the England captain's armband while at the Club:

David Jack, four times, 1930–1932
Eddie Hapgood, 21 times, 1934–1939
George Male, six times, 1936–1937
Alan Ball, six times, 1975
David Platt, twice, 1996
Tony Adams, 15 times, 1994–2000
David Seaman, once, 1997
Martin Keown, once, 2000

UNUSUAL MIDDLE NAMES

David **Bone Nightingale** Jack
Bob **Primrose** Wilson
Sol **Jeremiah** Campbell
Gus **Cassius** Caesar
David **Carlyle** Rocastle
David **Reno** Bacuzzi
Caesar **Augustus Llewelyn** Jenkins
George **Hedley** Swindin
Archibald **Renwick** Macaulay
Jimmy **Tullis** Logie
Michael **Lauriston** Thomas
Chris **Anderson** Whyte
Alex **Rooney** Forbes
George **Melton** Grant

DOUBLE DUTCH VISION

Feyenoord's massive De Kuip stadium, built in 1937, owes the inspiration for its double-tiered design to the Arsenal Stadium.

The 61,000-capacity venue was the vision of the Feyenoord president of the time, Leen van Zandvliet. At first, when he proposed that the De Kuip should have two tiers, the other directors were sceptical, but when they visited Highbury in 1934 they were totally captivated by Arsenal's West Stand, designed by Claude Ferrier and completed two years earlier. Not surprisingly, they changed their minds.

Another feature of the Arsenal Stadium also influenced the De Kuip design. The pitch at the new Rotterdam ground was raised by about three feet so that the angle of the stand seating could be reduced.

Feyenoord, incidentally, can claim an even earlier link to Arsenal. In 1921, a former Gunners captain, Bill Julian, was appointed as the Dutch club's first professional manager.

TED DRAKE'S MAGNIFICENT SEVENS (1)

On 14 December 1935 Ted Drake set an English record by scoring all of Arsenal's goals in a 7–1 trouncing of Aston Villa. He had a total of eight shots during the one-sided Villa Park encounter – the other attempt hit the woodwork! Here is a blow-by-blow account of Drake's Seven:

15 mins: scores from close range after being put through by Beasley.

28 mins: bursts through the centre after taking a long ball from Bastin, then fires home powerfully from the edge of the box.

34 mins: responds first to score with a rebound from close range after Beasley misses.

46 mins: somehow manages to keep the ball from running out, before converting from a tight angle at the near post.

50 mins: meets a Bowden cross to volley home.

58 mins: pounces on another rebound, this time coming off a Villa defender, to slot past the keeper.

89 mins: receives a crossfield ball from Bastin to drive into the net and complete Villa's misery.

ARSENAL TRADITIONS (2)

Clapping all four corners

Another enduring tradition which was first introduced under Herbert Chapman. When the Arsenal players first run out on to the pitch, at home or away, they line up and turn to applaud all four sides of the stadium, as a mark of respect to those who have paid to watch them play.

GO WEST, YOUNG MAN

Over the years, a number of former Arsenal players have moved on to ply their trade, either as players or coaches, in North America. Some were part of the exodus to the newly-formed North American Soccer League (NASL) in the 1970s. More recently, several ex-Gunners have represented Major League Soccer (MLS) clubs.

The Stateside trailblazer, however, was Bill Harper, one of Herbert Chapman's first two signings for Arsenal in 1925. He spent three seasons with a team called Fall River, before becoming homesick and re-signing for the Gunners.

The latest Arsenal man to head Stateside is Steve Morrow, scorer of the winning goal in the League Cup Final in 1993, who was a player and then a coach with Dallas Burn.

Here are a few of the ex-Arsenal men who took the Yankee dollar:

Bill Harper . . . . . . .Arsenal 1925–27 and 1930–31, Fall River 1927–30
Joe Haverty . . . . Arsenal 1954–61, Chicago Spurs 1967
Geoff Barnett . . . . .Arsenal 1969–76, Minnesota Kicks 1976–80
Charlie George . . . . .Arsenal 1966–75, Minnesota Kicks 1978
Peter Marinello . . . . .Arsenal 1969–73, Phoenix Inferno 1980
Brian Hornsby . . . . .Arsenal 1970–76, Edmonton Drillers 1983
Alan Hudson . . . . .Arsenal 1976–78, Seattle Sounders 1978–83
Alan Ball . . . . .Arsenal 1971–76, Vancouver Whitecaps 1978
Peter Simpson . . . .Arsenal 1960–78, New England Teamen 1978–80
Anders Limpar . . . . .Colorado Rapids 1999–2001
Gilles Grimandi . . . . .Colorado Rapids 2003*
Steve Morrow . . . . .Dallas Burn 2002–04

* Grimandi agreed initially to sign for the Rapids, but decided soon after arriving that he wanted to go back to France, so didn't actually play a game for the American side.

ROB'S RECIPES (1)

MULLIGATAWNY SOUP

This soup was popular with former Gunners goalkeeper David Seaman who, according to Arsenal chef Rob Fagg, is a bit of a broth man: 'David likes all soups but he prefers the thicker ones!' On FA Cup Final day, when the players get to choose their favourite dish, Seaman always opted for two bowls of lobster bisque.

INGREDIENTS

25g low-fat margarine
1 clove garlic
225g boneless chopped chicken
1 medium onion
1 green pepper, 1 carrot, 1 courgette, all diced small
2 tablespoons of plain flour
2 tablespoons of curry powder
1 tablespoon of tomato purée
2 pints of chicken stock

GARNISH

1 finely chopped and peeled apple
2 finely chopped spring onions
2 tablespoons of yoghurt
desiccated coconut

METHOD

1 Heat the fat
2 Add the garlic, chicken and vegetables, then cook for five minutes
3 Add the flour and curry powder, mix well
4 Add the tomato purée
5 Add the hot stock gradually, stirring all the time. Simmer for 20 minutes, stirring occasionally
6 Season and add garnish

FA CUP DOUBLES

Record signing David Jack became the first player to feature in FA Cup Finals for two different clubs when he took to the field for Arsenal in 1930 against Huddersfield Town. While at his previous club, Bolton Wanderers, Jack had scored the first ever goal in a Wembley FA Cup Final, the famous White Horse Final of 1923.

Just under half a century later, Brian Talbot went one better, becoming the first player to win back-to-back FA Cup finals with different clubs – for Ipswich Town (against Arsenal!) in 1978, and for Arsenal (against Manchester United) in 1979.

FIRST TO SEE THE LIGHT

On 19 September 1951 Arsenal staged their first major senior fixture to be played under floodlights, when they entertained Hapoel Tel Aviv of Israel. Previously, the only match for which Highbury had been lit up had been the annual Boxers v Jockeys charity match earlier that year.

Many in the game had been suspicious of such a new-fangled innovation. Arsenal, though, had been experimenting with the idea from as early as 1932 – yet another example of the pioneering spirit of Herbert Chapman, who installed lights at the Club's training ground after seeing them used on a trip to Belgium and Holland.

Shortly after the Hapoel game, which the Gunners won 6–1, this is what the 'Voice of Arsenal' had to say in the matchday programme on 29 September 1951. It sounds now like a prophetic vision of a floodlit future:

'We have, as you know, thought highly of the possibilities of this type of football and it was interesting to hear a remark from the terraces that a considerably better view was enjoyed than on a number of poor Saturday afternoons when strained eyes are peering into the falling gloom just before the final whistle.

'The floodlights, on such an occasion as this, would be invaluable. We are not suggesting that evening football should replace Saturday afternoon, for Saturday afternoon football is too much a part of the British way of life, and we are well aware, too, of the cost of floodlight installation; but we do venture to suggest that it could be well used to avoid a cluttering up of fixtures, which may accumulate through bad weather or a long run in the Cup.'

HENRY HELPS OUT

Thierry Henry is universally acclaimed for his goalscoring exploits. But, as the stats for the 2002/03 season proved, he is much more than just a top marksman. The Frenchman was credited with 20 assists that term, a Premiership record.

FAMOUS SCANDINAVIAN FANS

Erling Kagge – polar explorer
A pioneering Norwegian explorer, who became the first person in history to reach the North Pole, the South Pole and the summit of Mount Everest. A member of the first unsupported team expedition to the North Pole in 1990, three years later he completed an unsupported solo expedition to the South Pole. He also has a degree in Law and is one of Norway's leading publishers: 'Over the years I've sailed the oceans, skied to the Poles, climbed mountains and written books, but Arsenal have never been out of my thoughts!'

Bjarte Engen Vik – Nordic ski champion
Norway's former Olympic and World Nordic-Combined ski champion reckons he would rather have played for Arsenal: 'I was given an Arsenal kit when I was five . . . if I could have chosen between being a professional footballer for Arsenal or a combined skier, I would have chosen the Gunners.'

VG Newspaper, Norway, 1998

Lennart Johansson – UEFA President
The Swede ranks Arsenal second in his affections after AIK Solna. He has said that he tries to watch the Gunners whenever possible and that Charlie George is his favourite player. In an interview in January 1998, he told *The Independent*: 'Of course, you have Manchester United and Liverpool, but Arsenal are the best of the lot.'

King Olav V – former Norwegian monarch
Norway's king from 1957 until his death in 1991, Olav was, according to the Norwegian Embassy in London, 'a very keen Arsenal supporter all his life,' and he always sat in the Upper East Stand on his visits to Highbury. The nephew of Britain's King George V, Olav was born and educated in England, and was a fine sportsman himself, winning a yachting gold medal for Norway at the 1928 Olympics.

Jan Molby – ex-Liverpool and Denmark footballer
The Dane with the Scouser's accent plied his trade on Merseyside, but his heart has always belonged to Highbury. 'Arsenal were, and still are, my team. I am an Arsenal fan and have been since I was a child in Denmark . . . I loved Liam Brady . . . he was a genius.'

Total Football, June, 1999

Benny Andersson – Swedish songman

The one-time member of the Swedish pop group ABBA used to appear frequently in TV interviews wearing his Arsenal shirt and always kept tabs on the team's results while the band were on tour.

1971 FA CUP FINAL

8 May 1971 • Wembley • Attendance: 100,000
Arsenal 2 Liverpool 1 (after extra time) (Goals: Kelly, George)
Formation: 4-3-3

WILSON

RICE   McLINTOCK   SIMPSON   McNAB

ARMSTRONG   GRAHAM   STOREY

RADFORD   GEORGE   KENNEDY

Sub used: 12 Kelly (for Storey)

DERBY DAZZLER (4)

DAVID ROCASTLE
4 March 1987 • Spurs 1 Arsenal 2
Littlewoods Cup semi-final replay, White Hart Lane

Arguably the goal that launches the George Graham era. Deadlocked at 2–2 after a two-legged semi-final, the north London rivals had to meet for a third time. Having come from behind, Arsenal are heading for another draw before Rocky keeps his cool in the midst of a goalmouth scramble to slot home a last-minute winner. Arsenal go on to beat Liverpool in the final and lift their first trophy for nine seasons.

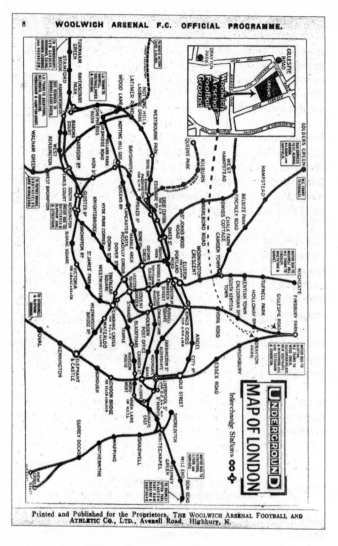

Printed and Published for the Proprietors, THE WOOLWICH ARSENAL FOOTBALL AND ATHLETIC CO., LTD., Avenell Road, Highbury, N.

A bespoke version of the London Underground map created specially for the Arsenal programme in 1913, just after the Club's move north of the river. Note the inset showing Gillespie Road, later renamed as Arsenal station.

HOW ARSENAL FIRST SAW RED

In the first year after their foundation, Royal Arsenal did not wear any proper kit. However, several of the players among that early squad – goalkeeper Fred Beardsley, Bill Parr and Morris Bates, who had arrived to work at the Woolwich Arsenal from the Midlands – were former players of Nottingham Forest, one of England's oldest and most successful clubs, and that connection led to a momentous change.

Ironically, it was Forest's success that steered Beardsley to London. In 1885, Forest faced the Scottish side Queen's Park in an FA Cup semi-final. The game, played in Derby, ended in a draw, and the replay took place in Edinburgh. Beardsley took time off work to travel north for the match, and was sacked as a result. This prompted him to move to London, where he found work as a turner at the Arsenal's Dial Square Factory.

One weekend Beardsley travelled back to Nottingham. Thanks to his connections at the club, he returned with a ball and some second-hand Forest kits – then, as now, Forest played in red. These were duly adopted as the new Royal Arsenal colours. The full kit comprised red long-sleeved shirt with collar and three buttons; white knee-length knickerbockers, and blue-and-white hooped socks made out of heavy wool.

There was a price to pay. Arsenal had to agree to let Beardsley continue turning out for Forest, and for a time he managed to commute between Nottingham and London, playing for both teams.

In 1891, Beardsley was elected Arsenal's vice chairman, and when the Club was transformed into a limited company two years later, he was one of the founder directors, doubling up as head scout.

IF YOU'RE GOOD ENOUGH, YOU'RE YOUNG ENOUGH

Leslie Compton holds the record of being the oldest debutant for England. The Arsenal centre back won his first full cap against Wales on 15 November 1950, at the tender age of 38 and 64 days.

GILBERTO THE GIANT ANTEATER

In 2003, London Zoo named a giant anteater after Gilberto, when Arsenal supporter Peter Findlay won a competition to sponsor the animal.

Like the midfielder, the giant anteater (*Myrmecophaga tridactyla*) is a native of Brazil. 'To be honest, I've never seen an anteater in the wild back home in Brazil, but it was great to meet Gilberto here. He can now be like a brother to me,' said the happy World Cup winner on a visit to meet his namesake at London Zoo.

When fully grown, Gilberto (the anteater) could reach 122 cm (4 ft) in length, excluding his tail, and about 61 cm (2 ft) in height, weighing approximately 50.8 kg (8 st). The Arsenal star stands at 192 cm (6 ft 3 in), tipping the scales at 80.3 kg (12.9 st).

BOXING CLEVER

A large number of boxing champions, both past and present, are Arsenal supporters, including:

Sir Henry Cooper, former British and Empire heavyweight champion
Michael Watson, former Commonwealth middleweight champion
Gary Mason, former British heavyweight champion
Jim McDonnell, former European featherweight champion
Audley Harrison, 2000 Olympic super heavyweight gold medallist and WBF heavyweight champion
Nicky Cook, European featherweight champion
Chris Okoh, former Commonwealth cruiserweight champion
Danny Williams, former British and Commonwealth heavyweight champion
Adrian Dodson, former IBO super middleweight champion
Takaloo, former WBU light middleweight champion.

The top boxing promoter, **Frank Warren,** is also a diehard Arsenal fan, and has an executive box at Highbury.

See also: Boxers and Jockeys (page 34) and Cooper v Ali (page 41)

ARSENAL'S FIRST TROPHY

The 1930 FA Cup victory is widely regarded as Arsenal's first real honour. However, their first major trophy was claimed almost 40 years earlier when they lifted the London Senior Cup.

The final took place at Kennington Oval on 7 March 1891, six months before Royal Arsenal turned professional. Playing in front of a crowd of about 6,000, they defeated the Medicos (a team from Bart's Hospital) 6–0, inspired by their flamboyant outside right, Albert Christmas.

Royal Arsenal line-up v Bart's • Formation: 2-3-5

CHAPMAN INNOVATIONS (4)

Playing by numbers

In 1928 Herbert Chapman introduced numbered shirts for the first time, in a fixture between Arsenal and Sheffield Wednesday. He also persuaded Chelsea to do the same for their match that day.

In Chapman's system, the home team took numbers 1 to 11 and the away team 12 to 22. The FA hated the idea, and made him drop it. Chapman, however, continued using numbered shirts for the Arsenal reserve team.

The FA finally came round to Chapman's way of thinking for the 1933 FA Cup Final, while shirt numbers in the League became mandatory in 1939.

Division One 1937/38

	P		Home					Away				Pt
	P	W	D	L	F	A	W	D	L	F	A	Pt
Arsenal	42	15	4	2	52	16	6	6	9	25	28	52
Wolves	42	11	8	2	47	21	9	3	9	25	28	51
Preston NE	42	9	9	3	34	21	7	8	6	30	23	49
Charlton Ath	42	14	5	2	43	14	2	9	10	22	37	46
Middlesbrough	42	12	4	5	40	26	7	4	10	32	39	46
Brentford	42	10	6	5	44	27	8	3	10	25	32	45
Bolton W	42	11	6	4	38	22	4	9	8	26	38	45
Sunderland	42	12	6	3	32	18	2	10	9	23	39	44
Leeds Utd	42	11	6	4	38	26	3	9	9	26	43	43
Chelsea	42	11	6	4	40	22	3	7	11	25	43	41
Liverpool	42	9	5	7	40	30	6	6	9	25	41	41
Blackpool	42	10	5	6	33	26	6	3	12	28	40	40
Derby County	42	10	5	6	42	36	5	5	11	24	51	40
Everton	42	11	5	5	54	34	5	2	14	25	41	39
Huddersfield T	42	11	3	7	29	24	6	2	13	26	44	39
Leicester City	42	9	6	6	31	26	5	5	11	23	49	39
Stoke City	42	10	7	4	42	21	3	5	13	16	38	38
Birmingham	42	7	11	3	34	28	3	7	11	24	34	38
Portsmouth	42	11	6	4	41	22	2	6	13	21	46	38
Grimsby Town	42	11	5	5	29	23	2	7	12	22	45	38
Manchester City	42	12	2	7	49	33	2	6	13	31	44	36
WBA	42	10	5	6	46	36	4	3	14	28	55	36

THE THINGS THEY SAY (5)

'Dennis Bergkamp controls a Ray Parlour cross with a lovely first touch which serves to deceive the defender, then he skips past the second one before picking the spot, the onrushing goalie is stranded. One-nil to thee Ar-si-nil.'

From Filth *by Irvine Welsh.*

AN EXTENSIVE AFC DISCOGRAPHY

I Wish I Could Play Like Charlie George – **The Strikers and Selston Bagthorpe Primary School Choir** (1972)

Dial Square – **Midway Still** (1992)

Your Arsenal – **Morrissey** (1992)

The Victory Song – **Enrico Cocozza** (1993)

Highbury Heartbeat – **The IASA Wembley Mix** (1993)

Arrivederci Liam – **Stephen North and the Flat Back Four** (1995)

The Gus Caesar Rap – **Stephen North and the Flat Back Four** (1995)

The Charlie George Calypso – **Stephen North and the Flat Back Four** (1995)

Arsenal Rap – **The A Team** (1995)

Gooneroonie – **The A Team** (1995)

Come On You Gunners – **Tina and the North Bank** (1995)

Ooh Ooh Tony Adams – **The A Team** (1995)

Come On You Reds – **The Arsenal Supporters** (1995)

One Night At Anfield – **Top Gooner** (1995)

The Only Cockney Rebel (That Meant Anything To Me Was Charlie George) – **The Half Time Oranges** (1998)

Tony Adams – **Joe Strummer and the Mescaleros** (1999)

Bob Wilson: Anchor Man – **Half Man Half Biscuit** (2001)

Vieira – **Jackin' The Box and Dj Fresh** (2001)

We Are Arsenal – **Wenger Boys** (2001)

Highbury Sunshine – **Yeah** (2001)

Mr Bergkamp – **Yeah** (2001)

Thierry Henry Song – **The Away Crew** (2001)

Thierry Henry – **Arsène Sings** (2001)

We All Follow The Arsenal – **The Away Crew** (2001)

Beautiful Goal – **Pick 'n' Mix** (2002)

A.R.S.E.N.A.L Up The Gunners – **Arsenal Choir** (2002)

Arsenal We All Love You – **Arsenal Choir** (2002)

Glorious Goal – **Enrico Cocozza**

We Are The Best – **Enrico Cocozza**

Perry Groves World – **The Ginger Nuts** (2002)

Arsenal – **Tina and the North Bank** (2002)

Sol's A Gooner – **The Vieira Boys** (2002)

TURNING PRO

Woolwich Arsenal played their first match as professionals on 5 September 1891. The opposition were Sheffield United, and the Londoners lost the game 2–0. This is how the build-up to the occasion was reported in the press:

> *Tomorrow, the Woolwich Arsenal Football Club enter their new enterprise, viz. that of running a strictly professional football team, when they open their 1891/92 season with the match versus Sheffield United at the Invicta Recreation Grounds, which should provide a very interesting contest, as last year the meeting of these teams ended in a draw of one goal each.*
>
> *The ground is now completed and is greatly improved. The raised ground outside the rails at the entrance end will give the spectators a much better view of the game than that hitherto obtained from that end, and will also afford additional accommodation. The teams to be encountered are a formidable lot, as our readers will have seen from the list of fixtures already published; but opinion runs high that the now famous 'Reds' will render a good account of themselves. A band will be in attendance from 2 pm, and will play selections before and after the match as well as in the interval. Kick off at 3.30 pm.'*

From The Kent Mercury, *4 September 1891*

GOD MOVES IN MYSTERIOUS WAYS

Chief Rabbi Jonathan Sacks and former Archbishop of Canterbury George Carey are both avowed Arsenal supporters. Apparently the two first met at Highbury when the Gunners were beaten 6–2 by Manchester United in a Rumbelows Cup tie in November 1990. When Rabbi Sacks was asked whether the defeat meant there was no God, he reportedly replied:

> *What it proves is that God exists; it is just that he supports Manchester United.'*

Many Arsenal fans might suggest that this challenges the conventional wisdom that God is, in fact, Dutch, and wears a number-ten shirt.

WOOLWICH ARSENAL

Formation: 2-3-5

Here is how Woolwich Arsenal lined up against Sheffield United:

BEE

CONNOLLY

McBEAN

HOWAT

McHARDY

JULIAN

CRAWFORD

McLAREN

PATON

PEARSON

GRAHAM

PRIZE FROM THE SCRIBES

Since members of the Footballer Writers' Association began choosing their player of the season in 1948, Arsenal players have won the award six times. They are:

Joe Mercer 1950
Frank McLintock 1971
Dennis Bergkamp 1998
Robert Pires 2002
Thierry Henry 2003
Thierry Henry 2004

Thierry Henry is the only player to have won the award two years running. Arsenal are only the second club whose players have won it three years in a row. Liverpool men took a hat-trick of awards between 1988 and 1990.

The award, incidentally, was the brainchild of former Arsenal player Charles Buchan, who went on to become a leading football journalist – he launched *Charles Buchan's Football Monthly* in 1951 – and was one of four founder members of the Football Writers' Association.

FOREIGN EMISSARIES

A number of early Arsenal players later found work coaching foreign teams in the first decades of the 20th century, helping to shape the game on the Continent and further afield. Here are a few who coached abroad:

Bill Julian (Arsenal 1889–92): one of Arsenal's first captains, he moved to Holland with his sons, and together they coached a number of teams including Maastricht and Feyenoord.

Fred Coles (Arsenal 1900–04): Coles went on to become a cricket and football coach in Gothenburg, Sweden, and then coached Hague in Holland from 1910 to 1911.

John Coleman (Arsenal 1902–08): Coleman spent a year coaching in Holland in 1927.

Thomas Hynds (Arsenal 1906–07): Hynds spent the latter part of his career coaching in Italy and then in British Columbia.

John Butler (Arsenal 1914–30): Butler coached Royal Daring FC in Belgium in 1932, and later took on the Belgian national team.

Wilf Copping (Arsenal 1934–39): The Gunners' 'Iron Man' moved to Belgium after World War Two, coaching first Royal Antwerp and later, like Butler before him, the Belgian national team.

See also: The Gunner who helped build Genoa (page 118)

JOY FOR ENGLAND

When central defender Bernard Joy lined up for England against Belgium on 9 May 1936 he became the country's last amateur player to appear in a full international. Later Joy went on to become a respected football journalist, a regular contributor to the Arsenal matchday programme, and author of *Forward Arsenal*, one of the finest books ever written about the Club.

FROM HOLLYWOOD TO HIGHBURY

When silent screen comedian Harold Lloyd visited Highbury in 1934, he set a trend. Since then a number of other Hollywood actors have been sighted at Arsenal matches, and many more are known to be fans of the Gunners. Here are a few of them:

Actor/Director	Selected filmography
Jackie Chan	*The Medallion, Shanghai Knights, The Tuxedo*
Kevin Costner	*JFK, Robin Hood Prince Of Thieves, Waterworld*
Freddie Prinz Jnr	*Scooby Doo: The Movie, I Know What You Did Last Summer*
Spike Lee	*Malcolm X, Do The Right Thing*
David Soul	Hutch in TV's *Starsky And Hutch*
Michael Moore	*Bowling For Columbine, Roger And Me*
Owen Wilson	*Zoolander, Meet The Parents, Starsky And Hutch*

1987 LITTLEWOODS CUP FINAL

5 April 1987 · Wembley · Attendance: 96,000
Arsenal 2 Liverpool 1 (Goals: Nicholas 2)
Formation: 4-4-2

LUKIC

ANDERSON O'LEARY ADAMS SANSOM

ROCASTLE WILLIAMS DAVIS HAYES

QUINN NICHOLAS

Subs used: 14 Thomas (for Hayes), 12 Groves (for Quinn)

THE BOOT ROOM

Boot sponsors of some of the 2003/04 first team squad:

Jens Lehmann	Nike
Stuart Taylor	Adidas
Ashley Cole	Adidas
Robert Pires	Puma
Freddie Ljungberg	Nike
Dennis Bergkamp	Reebok
Lauren	Puma
Thierry Henry	Nike
Ray Parlour	Valsport
Edu	Lotto
Pascal Cygan	Nike
Gilberto	Nike
Gael Clichy	Nike
Sol Campbell	Adidas
Kolo Toure	Adidas
Jeremie Aliadiere	Nike

THREE CURIOUS FACTS ABOUT JOHN DEVINE

Irish international defender John Devine made 400 appearances for Arsenal in all competitions between 1974 and 1983, scoring 20 goals. Here are three things you might not know about him:

- Towards the end of his playing career, he coached and played for East Bengal Tigers in India, and then spent several months touring the country by train and motorbike.

- He is a talented singer and guitarist, and back in Ireland has produced recordings for singer Dominic Mulvany and has jammed with the Dubliners.

- He was once married to a former Miss Ireland, Michelle Rocca, who later became the partner of music legend Van Morrison.

GROUNDHOG WEDNESDAY

Arsenal won the FA Cup eventually in 1979, but there was a point when just getting past the third round looked like mission impossible. Drawn against Sheffield Wednesday, then in the old Third Division, the Gunners needed a remarkable four replays to progress.

The teams met five times in just 17 days, with Leicester City's Filbert Street, where the last three replays were staged, becoming something of a second home. Arsenal finally overcame Wednesday with goals from Steve Gatting and Frank Stapleton.

6 Jan	1–1	Hillsborough
9 Jan	1–1 (aet)	Highbury
15 Jan	2–2 (aet)	Filbert Street
17 Jan	3–3 (aet)	Filbert Street
22 Jan	2–0	Filbert Street

These were the days before the penalty shoot-out. That meant, with extra time in the first three replays, the teams had to endure a marathon 540 minutes of football. It couldn't happen today. From the 1990/91 season onwards, FA Cup ties were restricted to one replay, with penalty shoot-outs deciding the issue where needed.

IF THE CAP FITS

Arsenal's ten most capped players of all time*:

Patrick Vieira	79 (79)	France
Kenny Sansom	77 (86)	England
David Seaman	72 (75)	England
David O'Leary	68 (68)	Republic of Ireland
Tony Adams	66 (66)	England
Thierry Henry	58 (70)	France
Pat Rice	49 (49)	Northern Ireland
Sammy Nelson	48 (51)	Northern Ireland
Terry Neill	44 (59)	Northern Ireland
Sylvain Wiltord	44 (70)	France

* Includes only caps won while playing for Arsenal. Career total is shown in brackets.

1979 FA CUP FINAL

12 May 1979 • Wembley • **Attendance: 100,000**
Arsenal 3 Manchester United 2 (Goals: Talbot, Stapleton, Sunderland)
Formation: 4-4-2

Sub used: 12 Walford (for Price)

HOW THE PADDOCK GOT ITS NAME

As Arsenal regulars know, the section of the Lower East Stand directly behind the dugouts is commonly known as the Paddock. This is not a unique moniker – several other clubs have paddocks too – but the story behind how the Arsenal Paddock supposedly got its name is a curious one.

During the post-war years, a number of leading jockeys were regulars at Arsenal matches, in part due to a close friendship with two of the Club's players, Jimmy Logie and Arthur Shaw. As guests of the two footballers, they tended to congregate in a group near the players' dugout.

During one match, according to Arthur Shaw, manager Tom Whittaker looked over to see all the jockeys sitting together, and was heard to say something along the following lines: 'There's so many of them there, it looks like a paddock!' And the name stuck.

See also: Boxers and Jockeys (page 34)

The following Arsenal men, past and present, have been awarded military or civilian honours:

Dr Leigh R Roose MM (Military Medal, World War One)
Dr James Paterson MC (Military Cross, World War One)
Charles Buchan MM (Military Medal, 1918)
Billy Milne DCM (Distinguished Conduct Medal, 1918)
Ernest North MM (Military Medal, World War One)
Ian McPherson DFC (Distinguished Flying Cross, 1944, and bar, 1945)
Alf Fields BEM (British Empire Medal, 1945)
Tom Whittaker MBE (1945)
Denis Compton CBE (1958)
Billy Wright CBE (1959)
Bertie Mee OBE (1972)
Frank McLintock MBE (1972)
George Eastham OBE (1973)
Joe Mercer OBE (1976)
Pat Jennings MBE (1976) and OBE (1987)
Arfon Griffiths MBE (1977)
John Hollins MBE (1982)
David Seaman MBE (1997)
Tony Adams MBE (1999)
Alan Ball MBE (2000)
Ken Friar OBE (2000)
Viv Anderson MBE (2000)
Ian Wright MBE (2000)
Arsène Wenger OBE (2003)

───── **THE PREVIOUS CLUBS OF BORO PRIMORAC** ─────

The previous clubs of Arsenal's first-team coach Boro Primorac:

As a player:	**As a coach:**
Hadjuk Split (Former Yugoslavia)	Cannes (France)
Cannes (France)	Valenciennes (France)
Lille (France)	Grampus Eight Nagoya (Japan)

CHAMPION GUNNERS (6)

Division One 1947/48

	P		Home					Away				Pt
		W	D	L	F	A	W	D	L	F	A	
Arsenal	**42**	**15**	**3**	**3**	**56**	**15**	**8**	**10**	**3**	**25**	**17**	**59**
Manchester Utd	42	11	7	3	50	27	8	7	6	31	21	52
Burnley	42	12	5	4	31	12	8	7	6	25	31	52
Derby County	42	11	6	4	38	24	8	6	7	39	33	50
Wolves	42	12	4	5	45	29	7	5	9	38	41	47
Aston Villa	42	13	5	3	42	22	6	4	11	23	35	47
Preston NE	42	13	4	4	43	35	7	3	11	24	33	47
Portsmouth	42	13	5	3	44	17	6	2	13	24	33	45
Blackpool	42	13	4	4	37	14	4	6	11	20	27	44
Manchester City	42	13	3	5	37	22	2	9	10	15	25	42
Liverpool	42	9	8	4	39	23	7	2	12	26	38	42
Sheffield Utd	42	13	4	4	44	24	3	6	12	21	46	42
Charlton Ath	42	8	4	9	33	29	9	2	10	24	37	40
Everton	42	10	2	9	30	26	7	4	10	22	40	40
Stoke City	42	9	5	7	29	23	5	5	11	12	32	38
Middlesbrough	42	8	7	6	37	27	6	2	13	34	46	37
Bolton W	42	11	2	8	29	25	5	3	13	17	33	37
Chelsea	42	11	6	4	38	27	3	3	15	15	44	37
Huddersfield T	42	7	6	8	25	24	5	6	10	26	36	36
Sunderland	42	11	4	6	33	18	2	6	13	23	49	36
Blackburn R	42	8	5	8	35	30	3	5	13	19	42	32
Grimsby Town	42	5	5	11	20	35	3	1	17	25	76	22

A CHANGE OF DIRECTION

Some careers pursued by ex-Arsenal men after hanging up their boots:

Brendan Batson	Assistant Secretary of the PFA
Albert Gudmundsson	Icelandic Minister of Finance
Denis Compton	Chairman of Middlesex cricket selectors
Ian Wright	National Lottery presenter
Alex Wilson	Masseur to Kent County Cricket Club
Anders Limpar	Proprietor of the Limp Bar, Stockholm
Frederick Pagnam	Coach to the Turkish FA
Ian Ure	Prison social worker
Chris Whyte	Chauffeur
George Cox	Coach of Sussex County Cricket Club
Bertram Freeman	Silversmith
Gavin Crawford	Groundsman at Charlton Athletic
Thomas Graham	Ferryman
Eddie Hapgood	Youth hostel warden
Archie Macaulay	Traffic warden
Arthur Milton	Postman
Kevin O'Flanagan	Doctor to the Irish Olympic team
George Graham	Tottenham Hotspur manager

A couple of curious careers prior to football also deserve a special mention: **Rami Shaaban**, goalkeeper (2002–04), was a mountain explosives specialist, while **Sidney Hoar**, a winger in the 1920s, made straw hats.

NUMBER CRUNCHING (5)

73,295: the attendance for the First Division game against Sunderland on 9 March 1935, and a record for an Arsenal home game at Highbury. The highest attendance for any 'home' game is 73,707, when the Gunners played Lens in the Champions League at Wembley on 25 November 1998.

OTHER ARSENALS (2)

Arsenal de Sarandi (Argentina)
Distance from Highbury: 6,919 miles

Founded in 1957, Arsenal de Sarandi hail from the suburbs of Buenos Aires, and for most of their history have lived in the shadows of more illustrious neighbours Boca Juniors, Independiente and River Plate.

However, they can claim the discovery of the famous Jorge Burruchaga, who went on to become Diego Maradona's strike partner and scorer of the World Cup Final winner for Argentina against West Germany in 1986. In 2002 Burruchaga returned to his roots to become manager. A year later he led Arsenal de Sarandi to promotion to the top flight for the first time in their history. In the 2005 Clausura, they finished in 6th position, their highest ever placing.

KEEPING UP APPEARANCES

The ten players who have made the most appearances in an Arsenal shirt in senior competition:

David O'Leary	722
Tony Adams	669
George Armstrong	621
Lee Dixon	619
Nigel Winterburn	584
David Seaman	564
Pat Rice	528
Peter Storey	501
John Radford	481
Peter Simpson	477

NUMBER CRUNCHING (6)

14: the number of consecutive wins clocked up by Arsenal in the League from 10 February 2002 – a Club record.

JUMPER FOR GOALIE'S POST

Goalkeeper Peter Goy, who joined the Club in 1953 from Scunthorpe, once claimed the distinction of being high-jump and long-jump champion of Lincolnshire and Scunthorpe.

A number of other Arsenal players achieved sporting excellence in various fields:

Alf Kirchen (winger 1935–43) also represented England at clay-pigeon shooting (1956–58).

John Mordue (winger 1907–08) went on to become one of the world's best at Fives, a ball game similar to squash.

Dr Kevin O'Flanagan (winger 1945–49) was Irish national sprint and long-jump champion, and represented Ireland at rugby union while playing for London Irish.

Niall Quinn (striker 1985–90) could have gone on to excel at hurling or Gaelic football had he not chosen to join Arsenal.

Alex Forbes (wing half 1948–56) played ice hockey for Dundee Tigers and a Scottish representative side before turning to football.

Joe Hulme (winger 1926–37) was an expert billiards player, who regularly hit century breaks.

Alex Manninger (goalkeeper 1997–2002) turned down the opportunity to become a professional skier in his native Austria.

Joe Wade (full back 1945–54) was a junior ABA boxing champion in 1938, and twice reached the London Federation of Boy's Clubs finals.

Reginald Tricker (inside forward 1927–29) was East Anglian hurdles champion for two years before taking up football.

See also: Cricketing Gunners (page 104)

INTER-CONTINENTAL CHARLIE

North Bank hero and local Islington lad Charlie George is the only Arsenal man, and possibly the only Englishman, to have played for teams from four different continents. Having left Highbury in 1975, George moved on to Derby County and then Southampton, but he also managed to fit in summer gigs playing for clubs in Australasia, North America and Asia:

- St George Budapest (Australia), 1977
- Minnesota Kicks (USA), 1978
- Bulova (Hong Kong), 1981

Eventually George came full circle, and these days he is to be found regularly at Highbury, where he conducts tours around the Arsenal Stadium and assists with matchday hospitality.

1993 FA CUP FINAL REPLAY

20 May 1993 • Wembley • Attendance: 62,267
Arsenal 2 Sheffield Wednesday 1 (aet) (Goals: Wright, Linighan)
Formation: 4-3-3

SEAMAN

DIXON   ADAMS   LINIGHAN   WINTERBURN

JENSEN   DAVIS   MERSON

CAMPBELL   SMITH   WRIGHT

Sub used: 12 O'Leary (for Wright)

Dear Sir,

I feel that I must write a few lines regarding Arsenal back in the Woolwich days. I've been an Arsenal fan ever since 1894, which was the year of my first visit to see them play as a lad of 17. With two other boys I walked from Orpington to Plumstead to see the great 'Team of the Talents', Sunderland, play Arsenal in a friendly match. It was the first time a First Division side had come south to play, other than in a cup match. Sunderland won 2–0 if my memory serves me right. Boyle (or Boyd), centre half for Arsenal, broke an ankle in a game which was a real thriller.

I was at Plumstead a few years later when Freeman had been transferred from either Burnley or Manchester City to Arsenal. He was top scorer at that time. I was also at Plumstead when Arsenal gained promotion and have watched them ever since. I assure you I have enjoyed every hour watching Arsenal play – I could speak about all of the thrilling matches I have seen 'til the cows come home!

Arsenal, to my mind, were greatest when they won the Championship three years running. It was the greatest team ever; but you have been great all the way from Plumstead, with the finest sportsmen in your team that you could wish to see.

Yours, Mr Jempson,
Orpington, Kent, December 1952

ARSENAL TRADITIONS (3)

Flowers in the boardroom

Since the days of Herbert Chapman in the 1920s and 1930s, flowers in the colours of the visiting team are always placed in the boardroom and the VIP lounge on matchdays.

'Punch' McEwan joined Arsenal as a coach in 1914, after a career as a defender with Bury, Luton Town and Norwich City. It was said he could walk into a room and reduce all present to laughter, however bad the atmosphere. Nobody, word had it, boasted a larger repertoire of jokes or monologues. Hence his nickname: he was funnier than an issue of *Punch*.

Famous for always sporting a bowler hat and bow tie, McEwan was best known for his skills as a scout. He was so secretive about his missions that, asked where he was going, he would simply answer: 'Up the line.'

His standard line when delivering a scouting report on a player he didn't rate was: 'I wouldn't pay him in washers.' 'Punch' McEwan died during World War Two.

THE SCORING BOARD.

The half-time scores of all the principal matches are shown upon the Scoring Board erected by the "Football Evening News" as below. The letter on the Programme corresponds with the letter on Board—thus, A 0 1 means that the first-named Club has scored 0 and their opponents 1.

	HOME CLUB.	Half Time	AWAY CLUB.	Half Time
A	TOTTENHAM		*v.* BURY	
B	WOOLWICH ARSENAL		*v.* NOTTINGHAM FOREST	
C	MIDDLESBOROUGH		*v.* CHELSEA	
D	PRESTON NORTH END		*v.* BRISTOL CITY	
E	ASTON VILLA		*v.* EVERTON	
F	BOLTON WANDERERS		*v.* BLACKBURN ROVERS	
G	LIVERPOOL		*v.* MANCHESTER UNITED	
H	NEWCASTLE UNITED		*v.* BRADFORD CITY	
J	NOTTS COUNTY		*v.* SHEFFIELD WEDNESDAY	
K	SHEFFIELD UNITED		*v.* SUNDERLAND	
L	FULHAM		*v.* BARNSLEY	
M	BRADFORD PARK AVENUE		*v.* CLAPTON ORIENT	
N	QUEEN'S PARK RANGERS		*v.* MILLWALL	
P	CRYSTAL PALACE		*v.* PLYMOUTH ARGYLE	
R	ENGLAND		*v.* IRELAND	

For many years, each match on the stadium scoreboard was referred to by letters, with no team names, so in order to work out which score referred to which match, supporters needed to use the 'legend' in the official matchday programme.

LIKE SON, LIKE FATHER

Alex James was what would be termed, in modern football parlance, a playmaker. The creator of countless goals, he scored few himself. So when, on 2 February 1935, he bagged three against Sheffield Wednesday – the only hat-trick of his professional career – it made big news on the back pages.

Wednesday's manager Billy Walker had made the mistake of telling his team to ignore the threat posed by James, and to concentrate on Arsenal's other forwards, which allowed the Scot freedom to roam.

James himself reckoned his hat-trick had been inspired by his 13-year-old son, who had scored four for his school team that morning. 'That's more than you've scored all season' rebuked James junior, and this, according to the great inside forward, had spurred him into action.

DERBY DAZZLER (5)

TONY ADAMS
4 April 1993 • Arsenal 1 Spurs 0
FA Cup semi-final, Wembley

With just nine minutes left on the clock and no sign of the deadlock being broken, step forward Big Tone. When Merson lofts in a sweetly executed free-kick, Adams is there at the far post to head home and send Arsenal into their second final of the season against Sheffield Wednesday.

THE THINGS THEY SAY (6)

'If you sat near him at a big match . . . you realised the intense earnestness of the man . . . I have never seen such concentration.'

A Daily Telegraph *reporter on Herbert Chapman in 1930.*

LISHMAN'S TREBLE TOPS

In the 1951/52 season Arsenal's inside left Doug Lishman achieved the remarkable feat of scoring hat-tricks in three consecutive home games. It was all the more impressive because he had only recently returned to the side after being out with a broken leg. His 'hat-trick of hat-tricks' remains a unique achievement in the modern game.

27 Oct 1951	Arsenal 4 Fulham 3 (Lishman 3, Holton)
10 Nov 1951	Arsenal 6 WBA 3 (Lishman 3, Holton 2, Logie)
24 Nov 1951	Arsenal 4 Bolton 2 (Lishman 3, Roper)

In the 2003/04 season Thierry Henry came close to equalling Lishman's record, notching up hat-tricks in two consecutive home victories (4–2 v Liverpool and 5–0 v Leeds United); the next home game, though, ended in a scoreless draw against Birmingham City.

— 1970 EUROPEAN FAIRS CUP FINAL SECOND LEG —

28 April 1970 • Highbury • Attendance: 51,612
Arsenal 3 Anderlecht 0 (Aggregate 4-3)
(Goals: Kelly, Radford, Sammels)
Formation: 4-4-2

WILSON

STOREY   McLINTOCK   SIMPSON   McNAB

KELLY   GRAHAM   SAMMELS   ARMSTRONG

RADFORD   GEORGE

Division One 1952/53

	P	W	D	L	F	A	W	D	L	F	A	Pt
		Home					**Away**					
Arsenal	42	15	3	3	60	30	6	9	6	37	34	54
Preston NE	42	15	3	3	46	25	6	9	6	39	35	54
Wolves	42	13	5	3	54	27	6	8	7	32	36	51
WBA	42	13	3	5	35	19	8	5	8	31	41	50
Charlton Ath	42	12	8	1	47	22	7	3	11	30	41	49
Burnley	42	11	6	4	36	20	7	6	8	31	32	48
Blackpool	42	13	5	3	45	22	6	4	11	26	48	47
Manchester Utd	42	11	5	5	35	30	7	5	9	34	42	46
Sunderland	42	11	9	1	42	27	4	4	13	26	55	43
Tottenham H	42	11	6	4	55	37	4	5	12	23	32	41
Aston Villa	42	9	7	5	36	23	5	6	10	27	38	41
Cardiff City	42	7	8	6	32	17	7	4	10	22	29	40
Middlesbrough	42	12	5	4	46	27	2	6	13	24	50	39
Bolton W	42	9	4	8	39	35	6	5	10	22	34	39
Portsmouth	42	10	6	5	44	34	4	4	13	30	49	38
Newcastle Utd	42	9	5	7	34	33	5	4	12	25	37	37
Liverpool	42	10	6	5	36	28	4	2	15	25	54	36
Sheffield Wed	42	8	6	7	35	32	4	5	12	27	40	35
Chelsea	42	10	4	7	35	24	2	7	12	21	42	35
Manchester City	42	12	2	7	45	28	2	5	14	27	59	35
Stoke City	42	10	4	7	35	26	2	6	13	18	40	34
Derby County	42	9	6	6	41	29	2	4	15	18	45	32

PARKER'S RUN

Between 3 April 1926 and 26 December 1929, Arsenal captain Tom Parker played in an astonishing 172 consecutive matches – every game in every competition for over three years. Nobody since has come anywhere near to matching that feat for the Club.

Nowadays it is rare for players to be ever-present for even one season. In 1995/96, David Seaman, Lee Dixon and Paul Merson achieved the feat in all competitions, but that amounted to a mere 47 appearances.

SOME LEFT-FOOTED GUNNERS

George Eastham
Liam Brady
Nigel Winterburn
Remi Garde
Edu
Emmanuel Petit
Ashley Cole
Silvinho
Stefan Malz
Stephen Hughes
Matthew Upson
Juan
Giovanni Van Bronckhorst
Robin Van Persie
José Antonio Reyes

WHAT'S THE ENGLISH FOR VA-VA-VOOM?

Not content with changing the face of English football, Thierry Henry is also busy changing the face of the English language.

Va-va-voom – the phrase made popular by Henry in his series of adverts for a certain French car manufacturer – has gained such wide everyday usage that it has been given a permanent place in the English lexicon. Authors of the eleventh edition of the *Concise Oxford English Dictionary* decided the expression deserved its own new entry, and came up with a the following definition:

Va-va-voom: the quality of being exciting, vigorous or sexually attractive.

CHAPMAN INNOVATIONS (5)

Rewriting the rule book

Many of Herbert Chapman's ideas, viewed as dangerous at the time, have since become integral parts of the modern game. Aside from being the first in England to advocate the use of floodlights and shirt numbers, he ▷

was also one of the early supporters of the white ball as a means of improving visibility during failing light. Like many of his brainwaves, this only began to gain acceptance in the 1950s.

It was Chapman who first installed a clock at Highbury's College End (now the Clock End). His was originally a 45-minute clock, but he was told to replace it by the FA, who feared it would put undue pressure on referees!

The Yorkshireman also suggested a ten-yard semi-circle on the edge of the penalty box some ten years before it was introduced. As further proof of just how advanced his thinking was, Chapman even mooted the idea of using artificial playing surfaces.

LEAGUE OF NATIONS

In 1995 Arsenal had featured players from just eight countries outside the United Kingdom and Republic of Ireland (Holland, Iceland, Yugoslavia, Sweden, Norway, Denmark, South Africa and Australia). By 2005, the number had grown to 34. The Gunners' all-time foreign roll-call includes 15 Frenchmen, seven Dutchmen, four Swedes and two Danes.*

France	15	Switzerland	2
Holland	7	Latvia	1
Iceland	5	Ukraine	1
Brazil	4	Lithuania	1
Germany	4	Nigeria	1
Sweden	4	Cameroon	1
Spain	3	Liberia	1
Denmark	2	Ivory Coast	2
USA	2	South Africa	1
Argentina	2	Egypt	1
Portugal	1	Libya	1
Norway	1	Australia	1
Faroe Islands	1	Austria	1
Croatia	1	Japan	1
Yugoslavia	1	Italy	1
Czech Republic	1	Zaire	1
Greece	1	Belarus	1

* includes players who have made at least one appearance for the senior side

MARTIN HAYES' UK TOUR

Former Arsenal midfielder Martin Hayes went on to play for clubs in Scotland, Wales and Northern Ireland. This makes him the only player, in modern times at least, to have featured for teams in all four parts of the United Kingdom.

- Arsenal (England)
- Celtic (Scotland)
- Swansea City (Wales)
- Cliftonville (Northern Ireland)

Later, Martin returned to the south east of England where he currently manages Bishop's Stortford of the Ryman Premier League.

STRANGE ENCOUNTERS

A selection of unusual football fixtures staged at Highbury

26 Oct 1938	England v Rest of Europe
3 May 1951	Metropolitan Police v Paris Police
30 Apr 1952	British Olympic XI v England 'B' Trial XI
11 Mar 1953	Floodlit Inter-City Football Match: London v Berlin
16 Mar 1957	FA Amateur Cup semi-final: Wycombe Wanderers v Corinthian Casuals
27 Mar 1957	British Army v Belgian Army
6 May 1960	England v Young England (an annual fixture at Arsenal for many seasons)
12 Apr 1965	London Hilton Hotel v Regent Palace Hotel
May 2000	Heinz Ketchup Schools Final: Barking Abbey v Ernest Bevin College

See also: Boxers and Jockeys (page 34) and Other sporting events at Highbury (page 11)

The Woolwich Arsenal programme on 6 September 1909 included adverts for
tobacconists run by two early Arsenal greats: Fred Beardsley, one of Arsenal's first
goalkeepers, and later a director of the Club; and Johnny Dick, a former Arsenal
captain, who had joined in 1898 and remained on the Club's books until 1912.

DENNIS BERGKAMP

To the tune of *Walking In A Winter Wonderland*

*There's only one Dennis Bergkamp
One Dennis Bergkamp
Walking along
Singing a song
Walking in a Bergkamp wonderland*

SHOOT-OUTS

Since the introduction of the penalty shoot-out, Arsenal have been involved in 13 such dramatic affairs, winning seven and losing six. Here they are:

European Cup Winners' Cup Final, 14 May 1980
Valencia 0 Arsenal 0
(Arsenal lost 4–5 on penalties)

Coca-Cola Cup, second round, second leg, 7 October 1992
Millwall 1 Arsenal 1
(Arsenal won 3–1 on penalties)

FA Charity Shield, 7 August 1993
Manchester United 1 Arsenal 1
(Arsenal lost 4–5 on penalties)

European Cup Winners' Cup semi-final, second leg, 20 April 1995
Sampdoria 3 Arsenal 2 (5–5 on aggregate)
(Arsenal won 3–2 on penalties)

FA Cup third round replay, 14 January 1998
Port Vale 1 Arsenal 1
(Arsenal won 4–3 on penalties)

FA Cup quarter-final replay, 17 March 1998
West Ham 1 Arsenal 1
(Arsenal won 4–3 on penalties)

Worthington Cup fourth round, 30 November 1999
Middlesbrough 2 Arsenal 2
(Arsenal lost 1–3 on penalties)

FA Cup fourth round replay, 19 January 2000
Leicester City 0 Arsenal 0
(Arsenal lost 5–6 on penalties)

UEFA Cup Final, 17 May 2000
Galatasaray 0 Arsenal 0
(Arsenal lost 1–4 on penalties)

FA Community Shield, 10 August 2003
Manchester United 1 Arsenal 1
(Arsenal lost 3–4 on penalties)

Carling Cup third round, 28 October 2003
Arsenal 1 Rotherham 1
(Arsenal won 9–8 on penalties)*

FA Cup fifth round replay, 1 March 2005
Sheffield Utd 0 Arsenal 0
(Arsenal won 4–2 on penalties)

FA Cup Final, 18 May 2005
Arsenal 0 Manchester United 0
(Arsenal won 5–4 on penalties)

* The author remembers this fixture slightly differently than most. Having
arrived five minutes late, he missed Aliadiere's opener, and with one minute
left, decided to beat the rush and make an early exit. Rotherham equalised
in the 89th minute, resulting in extra time and penalties. While everyone
else saw a dramatic 17-goal penalty-fest, he saw a 0–0 draw.

ARSÈNE WENGER'S LANGUAGES

French • English
German • Japanese
Italian • Spanish

STRUMMER ON ADAMS

'I realised that I didn't care about anything in the whole universe except for the fact that Tony Adams should be captain for the England football team. I am a Chelsea fan, have been since about 1971 or so. But when I look at him there's something great about the man.

'When you're watching a team on the field they also represent your culture, your tribe. Also, not a lot of people know this: he plays the piano. A lot better than me for instance, although that wouldn't take much. What I'm saying is that he's remarkable and shouldn't be taken for granted.'

The late Joe Strummer in Q Magazine, October 1999, explaining why he wrote a song called Tony Adams, released by his band, The Mescaleros, that year.

OTHER ARSENALS (3)

Berekum Arsenal (Ghana)
Distance from Highbury: 3,462 miles

Berekum is located in a small town near the Ivory Coast border, and the club's story is perhaps the most remarkable of all the foreign Arsenals. They were formed as an amateur side in tribute to their London namesakes, with Ian Wright as their official hero and the cannon as their emblem. A sign at the main entrance to their stadium proudly proclaims: 'We are the Gunners.'

Berekum Arsenal achieved professional status in 1996, and have since raced through all four divisions to reach Ghana's Star Premier League. In 2002 English Gunners supporter Peter Jones travelled to Berekum to present the team with 20 new Arsenal strips – a gift from Highbury – for their maiden season in the top flight, in which they finished a respectable 11th out of 16 teams.

PITCH IMPERFECT

When Arsenal played their first ever game, as Dial Square, on 11 December 1886, the Club had not yet managed to acquire a kit, so each player had to provide his own – and few of them matched.

The venue for the game, against a team called Eastern Wanderers, was a piece of wasteland on the Isle of Dogs. The Club's first secretary, Elijah 'George' Watkins, provides a graphic description of the playing conditions, which were, to say the least, a far cry from Highbury:

'Talk about a football pitch! This one eclipsed any I ever heard of or saw. I could not venture to say what shape it was, but it was bounded by backyards as to about two-thirds of the area, and the other portion was – I was going to say a ditch – but I think an open sewer would be more appropriate.

'We could not decide who won the game because when the ball was not in the back gardens, it was in the ditch; and that was full of the loveliest material that could possibly be. Well, our fellows . . . looked as though they had been clearing out a mud-shoot when they had done playing.'

The final score was, in fact, determined as 6–0 to Dial Square. The 11 men who played in that historic 'Arsenal' fixture were, in 2-3-5 formation:

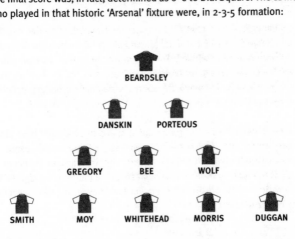

BEARDSLEY

DANSKIN   PORTEOUS

GREGORY   BEE   WOLF

SMITH   MOY   WHITEHEAD   MORRIS   DUGGAN

Between 17 November 2001 and 9 May 2004, Arsenal put together an amazing sequence of 29 unbeaten derby matches in domestic competition, including the whole of the 2002/03 and 2003/04 seasons. No other London team has ever come close to matching this feat.

2001/02

17 November ...**Spurs (a)** 1–1
15 December ...**West Ham (a)** ...1–1
26 December ...**Chelsea (h)** 2–1
23 February ....**Fulham (h)** 4–1
1 April ....**Charlton (a)** 3–0
6 April ....**Spurs (h)** 2–1
24 April ....**West Ham (h)** ...2–0
4 May ....**Chelsea** ....2–0 FA Cup Final

2002/03

24 August ......**West Ham (a)** ...2–2
1 September ....**Chelsea (a)** 1–1
14 September ..**Charlton (a)** 3–0
3 November ....**Fulham (a)** 1–0
16 November ...**Spurs (h)** 3–0
15 December ...**Spurs (a)** 1–1
1 January ....**Chelsea (h)** 3–2
19 January ......**West Ham (h)** ...3–1
1 February ......**Fulham (h)** 2–1
2 March ....**Charlton (h)** 2–0
8 March ....**Chelsea (h)** .....2–2 FA Cup sixth round
25 March ....**Chelsea (a)** ......3–1 FA Cup sixth round replay

2003/04

18 October ......**Chelsea (h)** 2–1
26 October .....**Charlton (a)** 1–1
8 November ....**Spurs (h)** 2–1
30 November ...**Fulham (h)** 0–0
15 February .....**Chelsea (h)** .....2–1 FA Cup fifth round
21 February .....**Chelsea (a)** 2–1
28 February ....**Charlton (h)** 2–1
25 April ....**Spurs (a)** 2–2
9 May ....**Fulham (a)** 1–0

Arsenal's sole defeat against London opposition during this period came in the home leg of the Champions League quarter-final against Chelsea in the 2003/04 season.

NUMBER CRUNCHING (7)

12: the number of goals scored by Arsenal against Loughborough Town on 12 March 1900 in a Second Division match, and against Ashford United in the first qualifying round of the FA Cup on 14 October 1893. The final score in both games was 12–0, which remains to this day the Club's record margin of victory in a competitive fixture.

STADIUM CAPACITY

The capacity at Arsenal Stadium during 2003/04 was 38,419. Here is how it divided up on all four sides:

North Bank Upper	4,180
North Bank Lower	8,191
West Stand Upper	3,839
West Stand Lower	6,879
West Stand VIP area	224
East Stand Upper	3,952
East Stand Lower	4,560
Press Box	78
Directors Box	146
Paddock	68
Clock End	5,795
Executive boxes	432
Seats for disabled supporters	204
TOTAL	38, 548

CHAMPION GUNNERS (8)

Division One 1970/71

	P		Home					Away				Pt
		W	D	L	F	A	W	D	L	F	A	
Arsenal	42	18	3	0	41	6	11	4	6	30	23	65
Leeds Utd	42	16	2	3	40	12	11	8	2	32	18	64
Tottenham H	42	11	5	5	33	19	8	9	4	21	14	52
Wolves	42	13	3	5	33	22	9	5	7	31	32	52
Liverpool	42	11	10	0	30	10	6	7	8	12	14	51
Chelsea	42	12	6	3	34	21	6	9	6	18	21	51
Southampton	42	12	5	4	35	15	5	7	9	21	29	46
Manchester Utd	42	9	6	6	29	24	7	5	9	36	42	43
Derby County	42	9	5	7	32	26	7	5	9	24	28	42
Coventry City	42	12	4	5	24	12	4	6	11	13	26	42
Manchester City	42	7	9	5	30	22	5	8	8	17	20	41
Newcastle Utd	42	9	9	3	27	16	5	4	12	17	30	41
Stoke City	42	10	7	4	28	11	2	6	13	16	37	37
Everton	42	10	7	4	32	16	2	6	13	22	44	37
Huddersfield T	42	7	8	6	19	16	4	6	11	21	33	36
Nott'm Forest	42	9	4	8	29	26	5	4	12	13	35	36
WBA	42	9	8	4	34	25	1	7	13	24	50	35
Crystal Palace	42	9	5	7	24	24	3	6	12	15	33	35
Ipswich Town	42	9	4	8	28	22	3	6	12	14	26	34
West Ham Utd	42	6	8	7	28	30	4	6	11	19	30	34
Burnley	42	4	8	9	20	31	3	5	13	9	32	27
Blackpool	42	3	9	9	22	31	1	6	14	12	35	23

RACING ACROSS THE CHANNEL

Between 1930 and 1962, an annual friendly match against Racing Club de Paris (now called Racing Club de France 92) became a traditional fixture in Arsenal's calendar.

Racing were one of France's oldest and most prestigious clubs. The encounters were initiated by Herbert Chapman and his counterpart at Racing, Jean Bernard-Levy, to raise money for veterans of World War One. Wherever possible they were played on, or near to, Armistice Day (11 November).

With the exception of 1932 and 1953, when the French team travelled to Highbury as part of a double header, all the games took place in Paris. The teams met 27 times, with Arsenal winning 19 of the games. The only interruptions to the sequence were between 1939 and 1945, due to World War Two, and the 1961/62 season when there was no fixture. From 1948 onwards the two teams competed for the Jean Bernard-Levy Cup.

Results of the Arsenal v Racing Club fixtures:

1930	Racing Club 2	Arsenal 7
1931	Racing Club 2	Arsenal 3
1932	Racing Club 2	Arsenal 5
1932	Arsenal 3	Racing Club 0
1933	Racing Club 0	Arsenal 1
1934	Racing Club 0	Arsenal 3
1935	Racing Club 2	Arsenal 2
1936	Racing Club 0	Arsenal 5
1937	Racing Club 0	Arsenal 2
1938	Racing Club 1	Arsenal 1
1939–45	No matches	
1946	Racing Club 2	Arsenal 1
1947	Racing Club 4	Arsenal 3
1948	Racing Club 3	Arsenal 3
1949	Racing Club 1	Arsenal 2
1950	Racing Club 1	Arsenal 5
1951	Racing Club 0	Arsenal 5
1952	Racing Club 2	Arsenal 0
1953	Arsenal 4	Racing Club 0
1953	Racing Club 2	Arsenal 4
1954	Racing Club 1	Arsenal 3
1955	Racing Club 3	Arsenal 4
1956	Racing Club 3	Arsenal 4
1957	Racing Club 1	Arsenal 1
1958	Racing Club 0	Arsenal 1
1960	Racing Club 4	Arsenal 3
1961	Racing Club 1	Arsenal 4
1962	Racing Club 0	Arsenal 3

NUMBER CRUNCHING (8)

7: the number of goals Arsenal scored in the away leg of their Cup Winners' Cup second round tie against Standard Liege on 3 November 1993. The 7–0 victory remains the Gunners' biggest win in Europe, and their biggest margin of victory away from home in any competition.

1998 FA CUP FINAL

16 May 1998 • Wembley • Attendance: 79,183
Arsenal 2 Newcastle United 0 (Goals: Overmars, Anelka)
Formation: 4-4-2

SEAMAN

DIXON   ADAMS   KEOWN   WINTERBURN

PARLOUR   VIEIRA   PETIT   OVERMARS

WREH   ANELKA

Sub used: Platt (for Wreh)

ASHLEY COLE

To the tune of *Gold* by Spandau Ballet

Ashley Cole, COLE
Always believe in your soul
You've got the power to know
You're indestructible
Always believe in . . .

THE FANS' CHOICE

Since 1967 the Official Arsenal Supporters Club has voted for the Gunners' player of the year. Two men – Liam Brady and Tony Adams – have won the award three times. Here are all the winners to date:

1967	Frank McLintock	1986	David Rocastle
1968	John Radford	1987	Tony Adams
1969	Peter Simpson	1988	Michael Thomas
1970	George Armstrong	1989	Alan Smith
1971	Bob Wilson	1990	Tony Adams
1972	Pat Rice	1991	Steve Bould
1973	John Radford	1992	Ian Wright
1974	Alan Ball	1993	Ian Wright
1975	Jimmy Rimmer	1994	Tony Adams
1976	Liam Brady	1995	David Seaman
1977	Frank Stapleton	1996	Martin Keown
1978	Liam Brady	1997	Dennis Bergkamp
1979	Liam Brady	1998	Ray Parlour
1980	Frank Stapleton	1999	Nigel Winterburn
1981	Kenny Sansom	2000	Thierry Henry
1982	John Hollins	2001	Patrick Vieira
1983	Tony Woodcock	2002	Robert Pires
1984	Charlie Nicholas	2003	Thierry Henry
1985	Stewart Robson	2004	Thierry Henry

WEMBLEY SING-SONG

Songs sung by the Wembley crowd before the 1936 FA Cup Final between Arsenal and Sheffield United:

- *Pack Up Your Troubles In Your Old Kit Bag*
- *Abide With Me*
- *On Ilkley Moor Baht 'At* (presumably just the United supporters!)
- *My Girl's A Yorkshire Girl* (ditto)
- *Annie Laurie*
- *Land Of Hope And Glory*
- *Love's Old Sweet Song*
- *Danny Boy*

DERBY DAZZLER (6)

KANU
5 May 1999 • Spurs 1 Arsenal 3
Premiership, White Hart Lane

A strike that epitomises the unpredictable skills of the big Nigerian. Kanu, his back to goal, controls a lobbed pass from Vieira on the edge of the Spurs box. Defender Luke Young is right up against him, but Kanu simply flicks the ball up and over his marker, then turns to collect and lashes in the Gunners' third goal to seal a vital win.

SUCCEEDING CHAPMAN

When Herbert Chapman died in 1934, Arsenal received more than 200 applications from candidates for the manager's job, including one from a woman. Some of the applications were on the bizarre side.

Perhaps the oddest of the lot came from a Welshman, who claimed in his application to have run a mile in three-and-a-half minutes, and who also offered his services as a player (either as goalkeeper or an 'extra fast and long-staying winger'). He wasn't shortlisted, and the job was offered to George Allison.

SWEDISH ODE TO A NIGHTINGALE

In the summer of 1931 Arsenal embarked on a seven-match Scandinavian tour. In a match against AIK Solna on 29 May, David (Bone Nightingale) Jack scored a hat-trick to help Arsenal to a 5–0 victory. His performance inspired famous Swedish poet and comic artist Jan-Erik Garland, who published under the name Rit-Ola, to pen the following poem:

> *David Bone Nightingale didn't run for his life,*
> *He was a strategist*
> *And a thinker.*
> *He could strike from all angles – direct shots and half-volleys.*
> *When he struck, he mostly struck 'cannons'.*
> *And Stockholm Stadium saw one of them 1931.*

For the record, the other results from the tour were:

14 May	Arsenal 2	Danish XI 0
17 May	Arsenal 5	Danish XI 1
19 May	Arsenal 1	Copenhagen Select 1
22 May	Arsenal 5	Stockholm Select 1
27 May	Arsenal 6	Swedish National XI 1
3 June	Arsenal 3	Gothenburg Select 2

───── SWINDIN'S NINE-WICKET HAUL ─────

On 2 August 1951 Arsenal took on Northern Polytechnic . . . at cricket. The star of the 12-a-side encounter was Arsenal keeper (and future manager) George Swindin, who obliterated the Northern Poly batting order by taking nine wickets for 20 runs.

Details from the scorecard:

ARSENAL

Cliff Holton lbw Norman	35
Freddie Cox b Lineker	53
Laurie Scott st Gage b Stovell	13
Colin Grimshaw c Gage b Lineker	28
Don Roper st Gage b Lineker	58
Joe Wade c Stovell b Lineker	6
Reg Lewis b Norman	2
Wally Barnes not out	13
Lionel Smith did not bat	
George Swindin did not bat	
Doug Lishman did not bat	
Peter Goring did not bat	
Extras	12
TOTAL (for 7 wickets)	220

NORTHERN POLYTECHNIC CC

TOTAL (all out)	113

Arsenal bowling figures:

Swindin 9 for 20, Lishman 1 for 22, Lewis 1 for 33

TED DRAKE BETWEEN THE STICKS

During a wartime match against Clapton Orient at White Hart Lane, Arsenal's legendary centre forward Ted Drake found himself acting as stand-in goalie. The reason? Regular keeper George Marks had phoned to say he would be late for the kick-off.

ARSENAL TRADITIONS (4): SUNDAY ROASTS

Since World War Two, a roast lunch has always been served in the Arsenal boardroom before Sunday fixtures. Normally, the choice lies between chicken and beef.

THE 70-MATCH SEASON

In the 1979/80 season Arsenal had to play a staggering 70 competitive fixtures, which remains a record in the English top flight and cannot now be topped. Their packed calendar was the result of reaching the finals of the European Cup Winners' Cup and the FA Cup, both of which were lost.

The FA Cup run included a famous semi-final epic against Liverpool, which took four matches to resolve, and the congestion was compounded by a run to the League Cup quarter-finals, with a replay in every round but one.

Here is a breakdown of the season's 70 fixtures:

> **Charity Shield** 1
> **League** 42
> **FA Cup** 11
> **League Cup** 7
> **Cup Winners' Cup** 9

THE 100 CLUB

Sixteen players have scored a century or more of goals for Arsenal in senior competition:

Player	AFC career	Total goals	Total games
Ian Wright	1991–98	185	288
Thierry Henry	1999–	181	298
Cliff Bastin	1929–46	178	396
John Radford	1962–76	149	481
Jimmy Brain	1923–31	139	232
Ted Drake	1934–45	139	184
Doug Lishman	1948–56	137	244
Joe Hulme	1926–38	125	374
David Jack	1928–34	124	208
Reg Lewis	1935–53	118	176
Dennis Bergkamp	1995–	117	392
Alan Smith	1987–95	115	347
Jack Lambert	1926–33	109	161
Frank Stapleton	1972–81	108	300
David Herd	1954–61	107	180
Joe Baker	1962–66	100	156

THE BATTLE OF HIGHBURY: ARSENAL 3 ITALY 2

On 14 November 1934 Arsenal made history by providing seven members of the England team for a friendly against Italy at Highbury. Never before or since has one club contributed so many of its players to an England starting line-up.

The 'Arsenal Seven' were: Frank Moss, George Male, Eddie Hapgood, Wilf Copping, Ray Bowden, Ted Drake and Cliff Bastin. Arsenal even provided the trainer for the occasion in Tom Whittaker. The match, a hot-tempered affair which ended in a 3–2 victory for England, came to be known as The Battle of Highbury.

2002 FA CUP FINAL

4 May 2002 • Millennium Stadium • Attendance: 76,963
Arsenal 2 Chelsea 0 (Goals: Parlour, Ljungberg)
Formation: 4-4-2

SEAMAN

LAUREN

CAMPBELL

ADAMS

COLE

LJUNGBERG

VIEIRA

PARLOUR

WILTORD

BERGKAMP

HENRY

**Subs used: 17 Edu (for Bergkamp), 25 Kanu (for Henry),
5 Keown (for Wiltord)**

SCORING, SCORING ARSENAL

Between 19 May 2001 and 7 December 2002, Arsenal established a new goalscoring record by finding the net in 55 consecutive League matches. The previous record of 47 matches had stood for more than 70 years and was set by Chesterfield in 1930 while playing in the old Division Three North, in an era when goals were easier to come by. The previous Premiership record had been just 25 matches.

In the process of achieving their feat, Arsenal also set another record, becoming the first team to score in every League match during a single season, in this case 2001/02.

The 55-match run produced 117 goals, 33 of which came from Thierry Henry. Four other players got into double figures: Sylvain Wiltord (18), Freddie Ljungberg (15), Robert Pires (11) and Dennis Bergkamp (10).

PATRICK VIEIRA

To the tune of *Volare*

Vieira, whoa oh oh oh
Vieira, whoa oh oh oh
He comes from Senegal
He plays for Arsenal

THE BRAZILIAN TOUR OF 1949

In the summer of 1949 Arsenal became only the second English team to tour Brazil (Southampton were the first). The Gunners took on seven of the great Brazilian club sides in less than three weeks. They started in impressive fashion by crushing Fluminense 5–1 in Rio, with Doug Lishman scoring four, but – weakened by the absence of several regulars from the first-team, such as captain Joe Mercer and the Compton brothers – they managed only one more victory.

May 15	Fluminense 1 Arsenal 5 (Lishman 4, Roper)
May 18	Palmeiras 1 Arsenal 1 (Logie)
May 22	Corinthians 0 Arsenal 2 (Lishman, Vallance)
May 25	Vasco da Gama 1 Arsenal 0
May 29	Flamengo 3 Arsenal 1 (Goring)
June 1	Botafogo 2 Arsenal 2 (Lewis 2)
June 4	Sao Paulo 1 Arsenal 0

Alf Fields, one of four surviving members of the 1949 tour, recalls: 'We learnt an awful lot over there. Their skill levels were very high. In many ways they were way ahead of us. They used a lighter-weight football, and played in much lighter boots. They used to give the players raw eggs in milk before training to help build them up, and they had oxygen cylinders in the dressing room. Another thing they did was to strip players down and turn the hose on them – the idea was that it stimulated the muscles.'

Arsenal returned for a second summer tour of Brazil in 1951.

SOME ARSENAL REDHEADS

Herbert Roberts
Alan Ball
Willie Young
Perry Groves
John Hartson
Ray Parlour
Freddie Ljungberg (henna-assisted!)

ROB'S RECIPES (2)

Banoffee Pie

From Arsenal chef Rob Fagg's extensive culinary repertoire, here is a big favourite among the squad, especially with Ray Parlour, Lauren and Freddie Ljungberg.

INGREDIENTS

- 2 x 397g tins condensed milk (unopened)
- 50g low-fat margarine (melted)
- 150g sweet biscuits (crushed)
- 4 medium bananas (sliced)
- 450g of crème fraiche
- Chocolate powder or grated chocolate

METHOD

1 Place tins of condensed milk in boiling water and boil for one hour
2 Allow to cool completely, open the tins and stir
3 Stir melted margarine and biscuits together to make the base
4 Press biscuit mixture firmly into a 10-inch flan ring
5 Refrigerate for 30 minutes
6 Spread condensed milk on to biscuit base
7 Add bananas and crème fraiche on top, and sprinkle with chocolate
8 Refrigerate for one hour, then serve

THE THINGS THEY SAY (7)

'Dennis Bergkamp is truly exceptional. His vision, class, range of passing . . . he is gifted; in fact he's a magician.'

Max Clifford, PR guru

THE ROMFORD FIVE

Romford has produced rich pickings for Arsenal in recent years. The following Arsenal men all hail from the Essex town:

- **Tony Adams**
- **Ray Parlour** (aka The Romford Pelé)
- **Stuart Taylor** (goalkeeper)
- **John Spicer** (who made his senior debut in the 2003/04 Carling Cup)
- **Steve Rowley** (Arsenal's chief scout since 1996)

JOHN JENSEN MANSIONS, HARLOW

Shortly after Arsenal's European Cup Winners' Cup triumph against Parma in 1994, an unusual monument to the Club's achievement appeared in Harlow, Essex. Four new blocks of houses were named after prominent members of the campaign: John Jensen, Paul Davis, Kevin Campbell and Ian Wright. It was the initiative of the Woolwich Building Society, a nod to the shared origins of the Club and the building society.

The original offices of the Woolwich were located directly opposite the Royal Oak, the pub where Arsenal's founders held the meeting on Christmas Day 1886 that helped determine the Club's future. The names chosen for the flats did not, however, prove very popular with the sizeable contingent of Spurs supporters in Essex, and were subsequently changed for fear of hitting sales.

THE FIRST FOREIGNER

Gerry Keizer was the first man from outside Britain or Ireland to play for Arsenal 1st team. A Dutch goalkeeper, he joined the Club from Margate, later to become Arsenal's nursery club, on 30 August 1930. He spent a season with the Gunners and made 13 competitive appearances, including one in the Charity Shield. But he was unable to maintain a first-team place and moved on to Charlton Athletic in the summer of 1931. Keizer went on to spend 15 years with Ajax, and won two caps for Holland.

Local sportswear suppliers H. Gradidge & Sons were regular advertisers in the Woolwich Arsenal programme. This advert appeared on Christmas Day 1909, for a League match against Newcastle United.

SIX-FIGURE RECEIPTS

In 1934/35 Arsenal became the first club to amass gate receipts totalling more than £100,000 in a season, contributing to an overall profit of £35,000. There was a quantum gap between the Gunners and the next most successful club of the day, Portsmouth, who made £14,961.

SEVEN MEN CALLED SHAW

Arsenal have had no fewer than seven Shaws on their books. They are:

- **Bernard Shaw** (1891–92): a forward who joined from hometown club Sheffield United and made just one appearance in a competitive match for Royal Arsenal in the FA Cup in 1892.
- **Walter Shaw** (1893–95): another forward, who played 19 League games for Arsenal, scoring 11 goals.
- **Herbert Shaw** (1898–1900): yet another attacker, who played 26 League games, scoring 9 goals.
- **Joseph Shaw** (1907–23): a full back signed from Accrington Stanley; later he managed Arsenal's reserve team.
- **James Shaw** (1926–30): an inside forward who arrived from Frickley Athletic for a fee of £100.
- **Arthur Shaw** (1948–55): a wing half who won a League title medal in 1953.
- **Paul Shaw** (1988–97): a forward who joined Arsenal as a schoolboy and went on to play for Millwall and Gillingham.

SIX OF ONE, HALF A DOZEN OF THE OTHER

On 21 April 1930 Arsenal played Leicester City at Filbert Street in an astounding match, which produced the only 6–6 draw in the history of English League football. Arsenal's goals came from Scottish centre forward David Halliday, who scored four, and Cliff Bastin, who bagged a brace.

Halliday's quartet was not enough to keep him in the side for Arsenal's next match, five days later – the FA Cup Final against Huddersfield Town. His place up front went to Jack Lambert, who scored Arsenal's second in the 2–0 victory that brought Arsenal their first major honour.

ARSENAL LANDLORDS

A host of former Arsenal players over the decades have gone on to run pubs or bars. Here are just a few:

David Jack ....The Camden Head, Islington
Charlie George ....The Ashley Hotel, Hampshire
Bob McNab ....The Spanish Rats, Tottenham
Willie Young ....The Bramcote Manor, Nottingham
Alan Sunderland ....The Halberd Inn, Ipswich
Lee Chapman ....So-UK, Clapham
Terry Neill ....Terry Neill's Sports Bar, Holborn
Anders Limpar ....The Limp Bar, Stockholm

Other former Arsenal players who later had spells as landlords include: Caesar Jenkyns, Hugh McDonald, William Bannister, Archie Cross, Andy Ducat, Horace Cope, Arthur Hutchins, Cliff Bastin, Frank Moss, Les Compton, Reg Lewis, Tommy Lawton, Danny Clapton, Peter Marinello, Alex Cropley, John Radford, Malcolm Macdonald and Ray Kennedy.

THE SECOND COMING OF CHARLES BUCHAN

In 1909 a local teenager by the name of Charles Buchan, who was on Woolwich Arsenal's books, fell out with manager George Morrell after he was refused payment of some sundry expenses. He left the Club soon afterwards and headed north.

Some 16 years later Buchan was to become Herbert Chapman's first signing and was installed immediately as Club captain. The newly appointed Arsenal manager wanted the 33-year-old so much that he persuaded chairman Sir Henry Norris to shatter his strict £1,000 transfer fee limit by paying Sunderland £2,000.

Arsenal, in fact, ended up paying out almost double that amount. In order to persuade Sunderland to sell, Chapman had agreed to shell out an extra £100 for every goal Buchan scored in his first season, a ground-breaking concept at the time. The new marksman duly delivered 19 goals.

ICELANDIC CONNECTIONS

- Arsenal have had five Icelandic players on their books over the years: Albert Gudmundsson, Siggi Jonsson, Valur and Stefan Gislason and Olafur-Ingi Skulason.

- Valur and Stefan Gislason, on Arsenal's books in the mid-1990s, were the first siblings to feature for the Club since the Clapton brothers, Danny and Denis, in the 1960s.

- The Iceland Official Arsenal Supporters Club celebrated its 20th anniversary in 2003, making it one of the Gunners' longest-established foreign fan clubs. It is also one of the biggest, with around 2,000 members – just under one per cent of the country's population.

- The Icelandic Supporters Club has its own website at www.arsenal.is

- When ex-Arsenal midfielder Siggi Jonsson broke his leg playing for Iceland against Scotland – the result of a tackle by Graeme Souness – he enjoyed the consolation of a visit from his favourite musician, Scotland fan Rod Stewart, who was in Reykjavik for the match.

- Siggi Jonsson has recently teamed up with ex-Spurs player Gudni Bergsson and Arnor Gudjonsson, the father of Chelsea's Eidur, to form an academy designed to develop the country's best young footballers.

- Arsenal's first Icelander, Albert Gudmundsson, joined the Club in 1946 before going on to play for AC Milan, Racing Club de Paris, Nancy and Nice. Later he became president of the Icelandic FA, Iceland's Minister of Finance, and his country's ambassador to France.

- In 2003 Arsenal's head groundsman, Paul Burgess, was invited to Reykjavik by the Icelandic FA to prepare the pitch for the Euro 2004 qualifier against Germany, after the local groundsman broke his leg.

- Nick Hornby's *Fever Pitch* has recently been translated into Icelandic and is among the country's bestsellers.

- Iceland's most popular musical star, Stefan Hilmarsson, is a massive Arsenal supporter, and has visited several times. The country's 2004 *Eurovision Song Contest* entrant, Jonsi, is also a lifelong Arsenal fan.

THE LEGEND OF THE HIGHBURY HORSE

Legend has it that there is a horse buried under the North Bank. The story dates to the 1930s when the Arsenal Stadium was being redeveloped. Allegedly, a coal merchant got too close to the edge when he was dumping rubbish into a hole on the North Bank and his horse and cart toppled in. It proved impossible to save the injured horse, which was destroyed where it lay and then buried in the middle of the terracing.

The story is a good one, but it is probably apocryphal. In 1991, when the terracing was removed during the building of a new North Bank, no bones, equine or otherwise, were discovered.

NUMBER CRUNCHING (9)

29: the number of goals scored by Ian Wright for Arsenal in as many matches in the League Cup, a Club record in the competition.

CRICKETING GUNNERS

Over the years, Arsenal boasted a fine tradition of footballers who also played first-class cricket.

Andy Ducat	Surrey and England
Wally Hardinge	Kent and England
Joe Hulme	Middlesex
George Cox	Sussex
Denis Compton	Middlesex and England
Leslie Compton	Middlesex
Jimmy Gray	Hampshire
Brian Close	Yorkshire, Somerset and England
Don Roper	Hampshire
Don Bennett	Middlesex
Arthur Milton	Gloucestershire and England
Ted Drake	Hampshire
Ernest North	Middlesex
Jim Standen	Worcestershire
Ray Swallow	Derbyshire
Ian Gould	Middlesex and Sussex

Ralph Prouton	Hampshire
Harry Storer	Derbyshire
HA White	Warwickshire
Ernest Stanley	Essex
Harry Murrell	Kent and Middlesex

MILK CUP FINAL

On the day of the 1936 FA Cup Final, an advertisement for milk appeared in The *Daily Express*. 'Train on milk!' urged the ad, below a photo of the Arsenal team, and an endorsement from the Club's trainer, Tom Whittaker.

'We are great believers in milk at the Arsenal,' affirmed Whittaker. 'I always encourage our men to drink plenty of it, but I recommend them to sip it very slowly. Taken this way it is easily digested . . . you cannot be undernourished in any way if you take plenty of milk. I believe it is definitely soothing to the nerves.'

Centre forward Ted Drake had clearly started his day with a glass of the white stuff. His cool finish in the 76th minute, despite a badly injured knee, ensured a 1–0 victory over Sheffield United.

THE ONLY LIBYAN TO PLAY IN ENGLAND

Signed from Italian club Prosesto, Libyan Jehad Muntasser played just one minute of one first-team match for Arsenal – a Coca-Cola Cup tie against Birmingham City in 1997 – though he was on the pitch longer than Jason Crowe*. Jehad rose from the bench during extra time, in the 119th minute, of Arsenal's 4–1 victory.

Later he moved on to Bristol City before returning to Italy and earning a place in the Libyan team. He remains the only Libyan to play in England.

Arsenal claim another Libyan connection, via former youth team member, Jay Bothroyd. Jay signed for Perugia in 2003, where he roomed and shared Italian lessons with Al Saadi Gadaffi, the son of the Libyan leader.

See also: Blink and you missed it (page 31)

CHAMPION GUNNERS (9)

Division One 1988/89

| | P | Home | | | | | Away | | | | | Pt |
		W	D	L	F	A	W	D	L	F	A	
Arsenal	**38**	**10**	**6**	**3**	**35**	**19**	**12**	**4**	**3**	**38**	**17**	**76**
Liverpool	38	11	5	3	33	11	11	5	3	32	17	76
Nott'm Forest	38	8	7	4	31	16	9	6	4	33	26	64
Norwich City	38	8	7	4	23	20	9	4	6	25	25	62
Derby County	38	9	3	7	23	18	8	4	7	17	20	58
Tottenham H	38	8	6	5	31	24	7	6	6	29	22	57
Coventry City	38	9	4	6	28	23	5	9	5	19	19	55
Everton	38	10	7	2	33	18	4	5	10	17	27	54
QPR	38	9	5	5	23	16	5	6	8	20	21	53
Millwall	38	10	3	6	27	21	4	8	7	20	31	53
Manchester Utd	38	10	5	4	27	13	3	7	9	18	22	51
Wimbledon	38	10	3	6	30	19	4	6	9	20	27	51
Southampton	38	6	7	6	25	26	4	8	7	27	40	45
Charlton Ath	38	6	7	6	25	24	4	5	10	19	34	42
Sheffield Wed	38	6	6	7	21	25	4	6	9	13	26	42
Luton Town	38	8	6	5	32	21	2	5	12	10	31	41
Aston Villa	38	7	6	6	25	22	2	7	10	20	34	40
Middlesbrough	38	6	7	6	28	30	3	5	11	16	31	39
West Ham Utd	38	3	6	10	19	30	7	2	10	18	32	38
Newcastle Utd	38	3	6	10	19	28	4	4	11	13	35	31

CHAPMAN INNOVATIONS (6)

Shoulder to shoulder

In 1930, for the first time at an FA Cup Final, the two teams – Arsenal and Huddersfield Town – walked out of the tunnel side by side. This was yet another Herbert Chapman touch, and it has remained part of the big day's tradition ever since.

THIERRY'S ALL GOLD

The 2003/04 season will always be remembered for the immaculate League campaign of the Arsenal untouchables. Thierry Henry's goals and all-round contribution to the cause were of paramount importance – a fact acknowledged in all quarters – and this was reflected in an unprecedented haul of awards to add to his Premiership medal.

- PFA Players' Player of the Year
- Football Writers' Footballer of the Year
- PFA Supporters' Player of the Season
- Barclay Premiership Player of the Month for January and April 2004
- French Footballer of the Year
- French Sportsman of the Year
- Runner-up in the FIFA World Player Awards and the European Ballon d'Or Awards.

TRANSFER MILESTONES

A century ago, four-figure transfer fees were unheard of, and at Arsenal they arrived later than elsewhere. Under the chairmanship of Sir Henry Norris during the first decades of the 20th century, a 'no transfer over £1,000' edict remained in place. Today, of course, even eight-figure fees are relatively commonplace. Here are the first Arsenal signings to add an extra nought to their fee over the years:

Four figures*	1925	**Charles Buchan**	£2,000	from Sunderland
Five figures	1928	**David Jack**	£10,890	from Bolton Wanderers
Six figures	1969	**Peter Marinello**	£100,000	from Hibernian
Seven figures**	1990	**David Seaman**	£1,300,000	from QPR

*The first four-figure transfer in England was that of Alf Common from Sunderland to Middlesbrough for £1,000 in 1905. Common joined Arsenal five years later, but the fee was only £250.
**Estimate.

TURKISH DELIGHT

In the summer of 1950 the Sunderland team were wandering around the Istanbul bazaars after completing their tour of Turkey. Entering a carpet shop they noticed that the walls were covered with Arsenal pictures. It turned out that the owner, one David Muhzud, was an avid Gunners fan, despite the fact that Arsenal had never been to Turkey and he had never seen them play.

When one of the Wearsiders suggested that the shopkeeper should change his allegiance to Sunderland, he reportedly replied: 'Why should I do that? Arsenal beat you 5–0 in December!'

Muhzud then produced a brass cannon – 16 inches long by six inches high – and persuaded Sunderland's manager, Bill Murray, to take it back to England and deliver it as a gift to Highbury. Murray duly obliged, and the cannon remains on display in the Arsenal museum to this day.

TURNSTILE TRIVIA

Arsenal Stadium has a total of 78 turnstiles.

North Bank 22
Clock End (Arsenal supporters) 8
Clock End (visiting supporters) 8
East Stand Upper 12
East Stand Lower 8
West Stand Upper 8
West Stand Lower 12

FIRST ON-AIR

- Arsenal's home match versus Sheffield United on 22 January 1927 was the first BBC radio broadcast of a football match; and Charlie Buchan's opener for the Gunners was the first goal that was ever captured for public broadcast.

- Later that year, in April, Arsenal claimed another radio first, when they faced Cardiff City in the first FA Cup Final broadcast by the BBC, which ended in a 1–0 victory for the Welshmen.

- On 16 September 1937 part of a match between the Arsenal first team and the Gunners' reserves was shown on TV, making it the first live televised game anywhere in the world.

- Arsenal also featured in the first match to be shown on the BBC's *Match of the Day* – a 3–2 defeat away to Liverpool in August 1964.

TWO STANLEYS V 12 DYNAMOS

In 1945, soon after World War Two, Dynamo Moscow embarked on a tour of the United Kingdom. When they touched down in Croydon, their list of opponents had not been finalised, but the Russians insisted to the FA that a game against Arsenal be included.

With so many footballers still on active service, the Gunners had to call on no less than six guest players, including the great Stanley Matthews and Stan Mortensen, which moved the visitors to complain that they were taking on an England XI.

The game itself was played at White Hart Lane in a pea-souper fog which limited visibility drastically. The Russians, controversially, insisted on providing the referee who, even more bizarrely, told both linesman to stand on the same side of the pitch.

There was yet more turmoil when, at one point in the confusion generated by the fog, Dynamo actually had 12 men on the field. The Russians won the game 4–3, Mortensen scoring two of Arsenal's goals.

ONCE, TWICE, THREE TIMES A GUNNER

Goalkeeper Hugh McDonald is the only professional player to have played for Arsenal in three separate stints (1906, 1908–10, 1912–13). Like so many of Arsenal's players in the early years, McDonald hailed from the west of Scotland. He ran a pub in Plumstead – near Arsenal's original home – until his death in 1920.

UNTIMELY DEATHS

Alexander Caie (1878–1914)
Spent one season as a forward with Arsenal in 1897 before moving to the USA. He was killed in a railway accident in Massachusetts, aged 36 in 1914.

Ernest Collett (1914–80)
A full back with Arsenal from 1933 to 1949, and later the Club's assistant chief scout. He died after being run over by a fire engine.

Jack Lambert (1902–40)
The famous Arsenal centre forward was a prominent figure in the Herbert Chapman era, and at one time he held the record for the most goals in a season – 38 in 1930/31. Later he managed Arsenal's nursery team at Margate before being killed in a road accident.

Andy Ducat (1886–1942)
Ducat, also an excellent cricketer, was one of an elite band of men to have won international honours for England in both sports. He died at Lord's cricket ground, aged 56, while playing for the Home Guard in a wartime match.

Robert Benson (1883–1916)
An England international full back who joined the Gunners from Sheffield United in 1913. During World War One he worked in a munitions factory, but accepted a last-minute call to turn out for Arsenal in a fixture against Reading on 19 February 1916. Lacking match fitness he was forced off the pitch through exhaustion, and he collapsed and died in the changing room.

Joseph Powell (1870–96)
A right back who joined Woolwich Arsenal from the army, and became Club captain, Powell broke his arm while playing for Arsenal in a United League match on 23 November 1896 and contracted blood poisoning and tetanus. His arm was amputated, but he died six days later.

Niccolo Galli (1983–2001)
Signed from Fiorentina in 1999, he returned to Italy on loan with Bologna the following year. He was killed, aged just 17, in a road accident in February 2001.

David Rocastle (1967–2001)

One of a generation of players who came up through the youth ranks, Rocky was a central figure in the successes of the late 1980s and early 1990s under George Graham, and remains an Arsenal legend. He died of cancer at the age of 33.

———— NUMBER CRUNCHING (10) ————

16: the number of players that were used by Arsenal in their 1970/71 Double-winning campaign.

———— ARSENAL IN BLACK AND WHITE ————

For one game only – an FA Cup sixth-round clash with Blackpool in 1953 – fans at Highbury, more than 60,000 of them, were treated to the unusual spectacle of seeing Arsenal turn out in black-and-white striped shirts and white shorts, in order to avoid a colour clash.

———— *VICTORIA CONCORDIA CRESCIT* ————

The Latin motto, which translates as 'Victory through harmony', was first incorporated into the Arsenal crest at the start of the 1949/50 season.

It owes its origins to the Arsenal programme editor of the day, Harry Homer (aka 'Marksman'), who, in his programme notes for the last game of the victorious 1947/48 League campaign, wrote: ' . . . my mind seeks an apt quotation with which to close this season, which has been such a glorious one for Tom Whittaker, Joe Mercer and all connected with The Gunners. Shall we turn for once to Latin? *"Victoria Concordia Crescit."* Translation: "Victory grows out of harmony."'

The motto remained an integral part of the crest in its various guises, until the launch of the new crest in 2002.

A K A

A selection of Arsenal nicknames:

Ray Parlour ....**The Romford Pelé** ....Samba skills in an Essex body

Dennis Bergkamp ..**The Iceman** ....For his ice-cool presence

Charlie George ......**King of Highbury** ....A local legend

Martin Hayes ....**Albert Tatlock** ....Coined by Charlie Nicholas,
who claimed Hayes sounded
like the *Corrie* grumbler

John Jensen ....**Faxe** ....A brand of Danish beer. JJ was
once doused in beer by his
Brondby team-mates during
post-match celebrations

Alex James ....**Old Baggy Pants** .....Due to his preference for
extra long, loose-fitting shorts

Tony Woodcock .....**One Chance** ....Coined by Brian Talbot for
the striker's claim that a good
striker needs just one chance
in a game

George Eastham ....**Korkey**

Wilf Copping ....**The Iron Man** ....For his fearless and
uncompromising approach
to defending

Liam Brady ....**Chippy** ....For his love of fried potatoes

Peter Storey ....**Snouty**

George Graham .....**Stroller** ....For his economy of
movement on the pitch

See also: Animal magic (page 19)

DIAL SQUARE BECOMES ROYAL ARSENAL

In 1952 Arsenal received a letter from an 84-year-old, Mr RB Thompson, one of the founder members of the Club and who played in the first Arsenal team. Not only did he feature at outside left in the first game against Eastern Wanderers in December 1886, he also claimed the first goal of the match – which ended in a 6–0 victory – by accidentally kneeing the ball into the net.

Thompson recalls the meeting, in December 1886, where the Club's name and colours were first chosen:

> 'These were settled at a hotel in Erith, after we had played the local club . . . we were a motley assembly. George Smith suggested we should have a uniform dress, and we displayed our shirts, jerseys, etc. These were all eliminated except two – a red shirt and a blue jersey with maroon band. On a vote the red shirt was chosen.

> 'Then the name was considered. Dial Square was the popular one, for five of the most prominent players worked there. Five others working in the Arsenal bitterly opposed this, and a seeming deadlock arose. I was the only member of the team not working in the Arsenal – I was a school teacher – and the youngest present.

> 'George Smith said: "We haven't heard what young Thompson thinks. What do you say?" Rather timidly, I asked: "Who outside Woolwich ever heard of Dial Square?" Followed by: "Who has not heard of the Royal Arsenal?" The name Royal Arsenal was adopted forthwith, and was later officially confirmed at a meeting at the Royal Oak, later in December.'

MONTAGUES AND CAPULETS

In a modern replay of Shakespeare's *Romeo and Juliet* in 2002, Darren, son of Arsenal vice-chairman David Dein, married Sara, the daughter of Spurs vice-chairman, David Buchler. Rabbi Katz, who oversaw the wedding ceremony, is a self-confessed Gunner. 'I am an Arsenal fan through and through,' he told *The Edgware Times*. 'I must have taken it in with my mother's milk.'

Down the years there have been other close links between the two footballing 'houses' of north London:

- During World War Two, Arsenal played their home games at White Hart Lane.

- Future Arsenal manager Herbert Chapman was Spurs' leading scorer in the Southern League in 1905/06, with 11 goals.

- Four men have played for Arsenal and later gone on to manage Spurs:

   Billy Minter (Woolwich Arsenal inside forward 1905–06; Spurs manager 1927–29)
   Joe Hulme (Arsenal outside right 1926–38; Spurs manager 1946–49)
   Terry Neill (Arsenal centre half 1959–70; Spurs manager 1974–76)
   George Graham (Arsenal midfielder 1966–72; Spurs manager 1998–2001)

- George Graham and Terry Neill have been employed as managers of both clubs, while Theo Foley and Stewart Houston have crossed the north London divide as coaches.

- Darren Baldwin, Spurs current groundsman, was previously the assistant groundsman at Arsenal.

- Vic Groves, uncle of another Arsenal player Perry Groves, played for both Spurs (as an amateur) and Arsenal in the 1950s, on either side of a spell with Leyton Orient.

See also: When Spurs bought into Arsenal (page 7) and North London moves (page 42)

NOT SO MANY HAPPY RETURNS

Since the Premiership began in 1992, ex-Gunners have returned to Highbury to score against Arsenal on nine occasions in League competition:

Kevin Campbell for Nottingham Forest on 29 August 1995
Andy Cole for Manchester United on 19 February 1997
Niall Quinn for Sunderland on 15 January 2000
Kevin Campbell for Everton on 21 April 2001
Paul Merson for Aston Villa on 9 December 2001
Nicolas Anelka for Manchester City on 10 September 2002
Emmanuel Petit for Chelsea on 1 January 2003
Nicolas Anelka for Manchester City on 1 February 2004
Paul Dickov for Leicester City on 15 May 2004

During this period, other ex-Arsenal men to score at Highbury, outside the Premiership, were former apprentice Ty Gooden, for Gillingham in an FA Cup fifth-round tie on 16 February 2002, and Lee Chapman for Leeds United on 25 January 1993 in the fourth round of the FA Cup.

ONE-CAP WONDERS

The following were Arsenal players when they made their one and only appearance for their country*:

John Coleman (England) v Northern Ireland 1907
Alex Graham (Scotland) v Northern Ireland 1921
John Butler (England) v Belgium 1924
Alf Baker (England) v Wales 1927
Herbie Roberts (England) v Scotland 1931
Bernard Joy (England) v Belgium 1936
Arthur Milton (England) v Austria 1951
Jimmy Logie (Scotland) v Northern Ireland 1952
Danny Clapton (England) v Wales 1958
Jeff Blockley (England) v Yugoslavia 1972
Jimmy Rimmer (England) v Italy 1976
Alan Sunderland (England) v Australia 1980
Brian Marwood (England) v Saudi Arabia 1988

Only includes UK and Republic of Ireland

NEW STADIUM FACTFILE

Some facts about the new stadium at Ashburton Grove:

- The stadium's capacity will be 60,000.

- The size of the new football pitch will be 113 metres by 76 metres, which is significantly larger than the Highbury pitch (only 105 metres by 70 metres).

- In total, the length of piles used will measure 30.2 kilometres, the equivalent in length to 300 football pitches.

- The heaviest piles at the new stadium will weigh 200 tonnes, the equivalent of 28 fully-grown African elephants.

- The amount of concrete being used for the piling foundations would be enough to fill ten Olympic-sized swimming pools.

- The steel placed in the ground for the piling foundations will weigh the same as 170 cars.

- The height of the new stadium will be 46 metres from ground level to its highest point.

- There will be 100 flights of stairs, which is enough to go to the top of the tower at Canary Wharf twice.

- The stadium complex will contain 2,000 doors.

- There will be 4,500 metres of metal hand-railing. This is the equivalent of two-and-a-half times the length of Oxford Street.

OUR WEEKLY CHAT.

BY THE DIRECTORS.

"Sirs, you are very welcome to our house. It must appear in other ways than words. Therefore I scant this breathing courtesy."

It is our pleasure to-day to welcome you for the first time to our new ground—a ground which, incidentally, is the most get-at-able in Greater London. That pleasure, great though it is, would have been greater had we been able to welcome you to a ground thoroughly equipped and laid out to its full holding capacity.

Whilst apologising to all and asking for their generous forbearance for such inconveniences as they must necessarily experience on this our opening day, we venture to think, when we state we have only actually been in possession for some sixty working days, that our patrons will admit we have got as near completion as has been humanly possible.

SECOND TO NONE.
On Monday morning work will be recommenced, and every day will add to the holding capacity and general completeness. It is our ambition that the ground and home of the Pioneers of League Football and professionalism in London shall be second to none in the Kingdom.

The accessibility of our new home is indisputable. It can be reached from the City and places adjacent thereto in less time than any other ground, and should, therefore, prove a great boon to the cosmopolitan enthusiast who finds himself in the City during the "kick-off at 2.30 p.m." season, when every moment saved in travelling is valuable. The quickest routes are fully set out in special details to be found on another page.

We are distinctly hopeful that, with the assistance of the football-loving public of North London, we may soon forget the depressing times we spent at Plumstead, with its poor train service and the lukewarm support received from those in the immediate neighbourhood.

We, however, fully realise that the ground is not the "all in all" of football. Play is "THE THING," and to be quite candid, our ambition in that respect is to regain our position in the First Division of the League, which we were unfortunate enough, through force of circumstances, to lose last season.

"'Tis not in mortals to command success,
But (with the assistance of the players—old and new) we'll do more.
We'll deserve it."

We desire to strongly emphasise one point. The Woolwich Arsenal Club has always enjoyed a deserved reputation for its high standard of football. Matches may have been lost, but it has always been the endeavour of the management that the players should play the game as it should be played. We have a keen appreciation for a good honest shoulder charge, but intentional hacking, bashing and smashing do not coincide with our ideas of sportsmanship, and those desiring to witness matches which are won by this class of football (?) must seek elsewhere. We want our visiting teams to look forward to a visit to our ground with feelings of pleasure (even though disappointed in the result of the match), and not with fear and trembling as to the possible effects of rough and unsportsmanlike usage.

OUR INTENTION.
The cost of laying out the ground and all other incidental outlays has not been a small item, and further heavy expenditure will be necessary before it is complete. We want to cover in the end of the field backing on to St. John's College in order to provide further protection against bad weather, and this we will do **if you will help us.**

The opening page of the first ever Highbury programme – for Arsenal's match against Leicester Fosse on 6 September 1913.

THE GUNNER WHO HELPED BUILD GENOA

William Garbutt, outside right for Arsenal from 1905 to 1908, went on to become a pioneering manager in Italy. His first club, Genoa, were among the early pacemakers of Italian football. As the English spelling of their name testifies (in Italian it is *Genova*), the club had been built on British foundations, but it was the appointment of Garbutt as manager in 1912 that opened the defining chapter in their history.

Aged just 29, Garbutt arrived at Genoa with no previous experience in management. But he became as important to his new employers as Herbert Chapman did to Arsenal. Quickly he introduced new training regimes learnt at Arsenal and his other clubs Blackburn Rovers and Reading, placing emphasis on tactics and physical fitness.

He assumed complete control of every detail, even insisting that Genoa installed hot showers in their dressing rooms, something previously unheard of in Italy. Also he orchestrated Italy's first paid transfers, first signing two players from neighbours Andrea Doria, and another from Milan. In addition, he organised the first foreign tour by an Italian team, taking Genoa to England.

Genoa's triumphs in the Italian championship of 1923 and 1924 were attributed directly to Garbutt's managerial wizardry, and prompted Italian coach Vittorio Pozzo to appoint him to help prepare the *Azzurri* for the Paris Olympics in 1924.

According to one of his former players, De Vecchi, Garbutt 'personified the archetypal old English gent, but was happiest on the field working with his players.'

In 1927, after 15 years at Genoa, Garbutt moved to became Roma's first professional manager. He went on to manage Napoli, AC Milan and then Spanish side Athletic Bilbao, before returning to his beloved Genoa in 1937 for another 11 seasons in charge.

Garbutt finally returned to England in the late 1940s. He died at the age of 81 in 1964.

THREE WILSONS IN GOAL

No fewer than three goalkeepers called Wilson have played for Arsenal, two of whom have featured in FA Cup-winning teams. Most recent, of course, is **Bob Wilson**, part of the Double-winning side of 1971, and later Arsenal's goalkeeping coach.

Then there was **Alex Wilson**, signed by Herbert Chapman from Greenock Morton for £600 in 1933, and a member of the team that beat Sheffield United to win the FA Cup in 1936. A subsequent career as a team physio eventually took him to the USA, where he worked in the North American Soccer League with the Boston Beacons in the late 1960s. He died in the United States, prior to the Arsenal team featuring Bob Wilson sealing the Double in 1971.

Their earlier namesake between the sticks was **Oliver Wilson**, who played one game for Woolwich Arsenal in the 1912/13 season, shortly before the Club moved from Plumstead to Highbury.

TED DRAKE'S MAGNIFICENT SEVENS (2)

A rampant Ted Drake plundered seven hat-tricks during the 1934/35 season, to equal Jack Lambert's Arsenal record of seven in 1930/31. The League record is held by George Camsell for Middlesbrough: he notched up nine in the 1926/27 season.

Drake's seven hat-tricks:

1 Sept 1934	v Liverpool	3 goals
29 Sept 1934	v Birmingham	4 goals
20 Oct 1934	v Spurs	3 goals
24 Nov 1934	v Chelsea	4 goals
1 Dec 1934	v Wolves	4 goals
15 Dec 1934	v Leicester City	3 goals
19 Apr 1935	v Middlesbrough	4 goals

--------------- **ALL WHITE ON THE NIGHT** ---------------

Extract from the programme for a floodlit charity match against Hibs on 22 October 1952:

The White Footballs

Messrs Stuart Sturridge & Co Ltd have kindly presented two white footballs which will be used in tonight's match. They will later be autographed and then auctioned, the proceeds being devoted to the National Playing Fields Association. These footballs are a new type, all leather and specially dressed to make them waterproof.

The white football was first used in England in 1932 when a London XI, including players from Arsenal, defeated a Rest of the League XI 3–0 at White City. Every time the ball went out of play, it had to be washed before being allowed back on the pitch.

The white balls only began to gain wider usage in the early 1950s, coinciding with the spread of floodlights, and were initially reserved for evening games. However, they were an instant hit with the fans who, when light became poor during daytime matches, would start to chant: 'White football, white football.'

--------------- **CUP FINAL KIDOLOGY FROM MERCER** ---------------

After he joined Arsenal from Everton in 1946, Gunners captain Joe Mercer continued to commute from his home in Hoylake in Merseyside, and would often train with the Liverpool team during the week. Liverpool, though, were Arsenal's FA Cup Final opponents in 1950, and a few days before the game, understandably enough, the invitation to train was politely suspended.

However, that didn't stop Mercer from indulging in a spot of pre-match psychology. As he explained, 'Whenever I bumped into the Liverpool players I told them they were certain to beat us in the Final. I fostered their confidence and it gave us an advantage.'

Division One 1990/91

	P			Home					Away			
	P	W	D	L	F	A	W	D	L	F	A	Pt
Arsenal	**38**	**15**	**4**	**0**	**51**	**10**	**9**	**9**	**1**	**23**	**8**	**83***
Liverpool	38	14	3	2	42	13	9	4	6	35	27	76
Crystal Palace	38	11	6	2	26	17	9	3	7	24	24	69
Leeds Utd	38	12	2	5	46	23	7	5	7	19	24	64
Manchester City	38	12	3	4	35	25	5	8	6	29	28	62
Manchester Utd	38	11	4	4	34	17	5	8	6	24	28	59*
Wimbledon	38	8	6	5	28	22	6	8	5	25	24	56
Nott'm Forest	38	11	4	4	42	21	3	8	8	23	29	54
Everton	38	9	5	5	26	15	4	7	8	24	31	51
Tottenham H	38	8	9	2	35	22	3	7	9	16	28	49
Chelsea	38	10	6	3	33	25	3	4	12	25	44	49
QPR	38	8	5	6	27	22	4	5	10	17	31	46
Sheffield Utd	38	9	3	7	23	23	4	4	11	13	32	46
Southampton	38	9	6	4	33	22	3	3	13	25	47	45
Norwich City	38	9	3	7	27	32	4	3	12	14	32	45
Coventry City	38	10	6	3	30	16	1	5	13	12	33	44
Aston Villa	38	7	9	3	29	25	2	5	12	17	33	41
Luton Town	38	7	5	7	22	18	3	2	14	20	43	37
Sunderland	38	6	6	7	15	16	2	4	13	23	44	34
Derby County	38	3	8	8	25	36	2	1	16	12	39	24

*Arsenal had two points deducted, and Manchester United had one point deducted, both for
disciplinary reasons.*

THE THINGS THEY SAY (8)

*'Singly, we can be broken down; together,
nothing can break us.'*

Jack Crayston, Arsenal right half in the 1930s.

FIRST TIME IN YELLOW

The FA Cup Final against Liverpool in 1950 saw Arsenal don an 'away' strip for the first time, as both teams abandoned their usual red shirts. Arsenal manager Tom Whittaker suggested a gold shirt with white collars and shorts for the occasion, an early prototype of the yellow away kit of future years. Keeper George Swindin meanwhile wore a bright red jersey for the game. Curiously, during the rest of the 1950s, Arsenal's regular second kit was based on white rather than yellow.

See also: Arsenal in black and white (page 111)

DERBY DAZZLER (7)

ROBERT PIRES
31 March 2001 • Arsenal 2 Spurs 0
Premiership, Highbury

Pires seals a 2–0 victory at the Lane, with an absolute scorcher from outside the box. Drifting in from the left in his inimitable fashion, he curls the ball past Neil Sullivan into the corner of the net. The goal is made poignant by the fact that the Frenchman dedicates it to another great Arsenal number seven, David Rocastle, who, tragically, had died earlier that day.

JUST NOT CRICKET

The manager of the Indian national football team, Stephen Constantine, happens to be a diehard Arsenal supporter, so when he brought his side on a tour of England in 2002, he arranged for them to attend a match at Highbury (a 5–2 victory against West Bromwich Albion).

'Arsenal were great' Constantine was to recall later. 'They even announced our presence over the PA. The only problem was that the announcer told the crowd that we were the Indian cricket team. Our captain, Baichung Buthia, turned round to me in amazement and said: "Isn't that a coincidence? They're here too!"'

During the 2003/04 season Arsenal actually had a Test side from the Sub-Continent in the stands, when the touring Sri Lankans attended a match.

HAPGOOD'S FIRST DAY

On 22 October 1927 Eddie Hapgood, future Arsenal and England captain, travelled to London from his home in Kettering to play his first game for the Club, against Chelsea reserves.

On the train to St Pancras, he met a man who regaled him with tales of his recent travels in Russia, and then produced a pack of cards, suggesting a game. The game turned out to be Find The Lady, and Hapgood agreed to have a flutter. Another stranger also had a few bets, while the rest of the passengers looked on. Then, suddenly, all of the other passengers left the train together.

When Hapgood finally arrived in London, he checked his wallet and found that everything in it, including his £10-signing on fee from Arsenal, had disappeared. He had been the victim of a planned set-up. 'It is the only time I've ever tried to Find The Lady,' he recalled later.

See also: Hapgood gets an armed escort to Spurs (page 138)

See also: Hapgood gets an armed escort to Spurs (page 138)

1993 COCA-COLA CUP FINAL

18 April 1993 • Wembley • Attendance: 74,007
Arsenal 2 Sheffield Wednesday 1 (Goals: Merson, Morrow)
Formation: 4-4-2

SEAMAN

O'LEARY

ADAMS

LINIGHAN

WINTERBURN

PARLOUR

DAVIS

MORROW

MERSON

CAMPBELL

WRIGHT

THE ARSENAL STADIUM MYSTERY

Filmed in the summer of 1939 and directed by Thorold Dickenson, the plot of this 'brisk little mystery' centres on the murder of a young footballer, Jack Dyce, who drops dead during a match between Arsenal and an amateur team called The Trojans.

The film, which was shot at Ealing Studios, incorporated real match footage from the previous season's home game against Brentford on 6 May 1939, the last official game before World War Two broke out.

Leslie Banks, a prominent movie star of the day, played the lead role – the Scotland Yard sleuth sent in to solve the crime – while Swedish starlet Greta Gynt provided the romantic interest. A number of the players were given parts, and even manager George Allison and trainer Tom Whittaker agreed to cameo roles.

Rookie centre-half Alf Fields was among the Arsenal extras who were asked to take part in the film. He recalls: 'Bernard Joy was the first-choice centre half, but he was injured. The next choice would have been Leslie Compton, but he was off playing cricket. So I was chosen, and they even gave me four lines to say. They were filming *The Thief Of Baghdad* . . . on one side of us, and a war film on the other, so the place was full of harem girls and soldiers.'

See also: Spanish puzzle (page 8) and Screen shots (page 132)

THE WORLD'S BIGGEST ARSENAL FAN?

When the King of Tonga, Taufa'ahau Tupou IV, decided to visit Highbury for a match during a state visit to the UK in the 1970s, special ad hoc arrangements were required. Being a man of some considerable girth, the King was provided with two seats in the directors' box, with the armrest in between being temporarily removed for the occasion.

ST TOTTERINGHAM'S DAY

St Totteringham's Day is the name given by Arsenal fans to the day in the season when it becomes mathematically impossible for Spurs to finish above the Gunners in the League. Although a moveable feast, in recent years it has tended to fall in March.

St Totteringham's day since the start of the Premiership:

Season	St Totteringham's day	Number of Arsenal games needed
1992/93	Spurs finished above Arsenal	
1993/94	26 March	34 (42 games in total)
1994/95	Spurs finished above Arsenal	
1995/96	5 May	38 (38)
1996/97	5 April	33 (38)
1997/98	28 March	29 (38)
1998/99	6 April	32 (38)
1999/00	16 April	32 (38)
2000/01	17 April	33 (38)
2001/02	18 March	30 (38)
2002/03	24 March	31 (38)
2003/04	13 March	28 (38)

THE *TITANIC* DISASTER FUND

On the evening of 29 April 1912, some 5,000 fans were at White City Stadium to watch a match between Woolwich Arsenal and Tottenham Hotspur, organised to raise money for the Lord Mayor of London's *Titanic* Disaster Fund.

The fund was set up to aid the families of those who drowned when the *Titanic* sank earlier that month. The match produced receipts of more than £100. Almost a century later, a programme from the match fetched £4,600 at auction.

HEAD TENNIS AT THE LONDON PALLADIUM

The game of head tennis was first devised by Herbert Chapman and Tom Whittaker in the 1930s, when it was, as it is today, a popular part of the training routine. During that era the games, normally three-a-side, were played on a specially built court, next to the stadium.

One day, a former Arsenal captain, Billy Blyth, came up with the idea of turning it into a stage act during the summer break, and he arranged for the Club's six best head tennis players – Eddie Hapgood, Ted Drake, George Male, the Compton brothers and Cliff Bastin – to put on a demonstration at the Palladium, London's top entertainment venue.

The theatre's two impresarios, Sir Oswald Stoll and George Black, were so impressed that they offered to sign the six Gunners for a collective fee of £100 a week, a huge amount at the time, given that the standard weekly wage for players in the off-season was £6.

Arsenal's head tennis stars were also provisionally signed up to take the show on the road, touring Butlin's holiday camps. However, there were delays in sorting out the details, and when war broke out in 1939, the idea had to be shelved.

RICH PICKINGS ON THE ROAD

The following five venues have proved the most productive for Arsenal in terms of League goals scored, up to the end of the 2003/04 season:

Venue	Matches	Goals
Villa Park	76	106
Goodison Park	84	104
White Hart Lane	68	100
Filbert Street/		
Walkers Stadium	58	92
Stamford Bridge	68	90

For the record, Villa Park has been the scene of another 18 goals in cup games – five against Aston Villa, and another 13 when the stadium was the neutral venue for semi-final encounters and cup replays.

EDDIE HAPGOOD'S FIVE CARDINAL SINS

In 1945 Eddie Hapgood gave a glimpse into his, and Arsenal's, success on the pitch with a list of the things a footballer should avoid at all costs:

- Wrong meals on the day of a match
  - Ill-fitting boots
- Lack of protection for the shins
  - Wrong heading of the ball
- Selfishness and lack of team spirit

CHAMPION GUNNERS (11)

Premiership 1997/98

| | | | Home | | | | Away | | | | |
	P	W	D	L	F	A	W	D	L	F	A	Pt
Arsenal	**38**	**15**	**2**	**2**	**43**	**10**	**8**	**7**	**4**	**25**	**23**	**78**
Manchester Utd	38	13	4	2	42	9	10	4	5	31	17	77
Liverpool	38	13	2	4	42	16	5	9	5	26	26	65
Chelsea	38	13	2	4	37	14	7	1	11	34	29	63
Leeds Utd	38	9	5	5	31	21	8	3	8	26	25	59
Blackburn R	38	11	4	4	40	26	5	6	8	17	26	58
Aston Villa	38	9	3	7	26	24	8	3	8	23	24	57
West Ham Utd	38	13	4	2	40	18	3	4	12	16	39	56
Derby County	38	12	3	4	33	18	4	4	11	19	31	55
Leicester City	38	6	10	3	21	15	7	4	8	30	26	53
Coventry City	38	8	9	2	26	17	4	7	8	20	27	52
Southampton	38	10	1	8	28	23	4	5	10	22	32	48
Newcastle Utd	38	8	5	6	22	20	3	6	10	13	24	44
Tottenham H	38	7	8	4	23	22	4	3	12	21	34	44
Wimbledon	38	5	6	8	18	25	5	8	6	16	21	44
Sheffield Wed	38	9	5	5	30	26	3	3	13	22	41	44
Everton	38	7	5	7	25	27	2	8	9	16	29	40
Bolton W	38	7	8	4	25	22	2	5	12	16	39	40
Barnsley	38	7	4	8	25	35	3	1	15	12	47	35
Crystal Palace	38	2	5	12	15	39	6	4	9	22	32	33

THE STORY OF THE ARSENAL CLUB CREST

The famous cannon crest was first adopted by Royal Arsenal FC in 1888. Originally, the Club's insignia boasted three vertical cannons, borrowed from the Borough of Woolwich coat of arms – a reference to the central role played by the military and the munitions industry in the area.

When the Woolwich Arsenal moved north of the river in 1913, and became simply Arsenal, the cannon disappeared from the Club's iconography for almost a decade, only to resurface in new guise at the start of the 1922/23 season, as just one cannon, pointing east.

In 1925, a narrower, more stylised cannon appeared, this time pointing west, as it continued to do for the next 77 years. At this point the legend 'The Gunners' appeared for the first time, although this later disappeared.

The next major development came in 1949, when a more complex crest was embraced. This incorporated the cannon, the Club name in gothic lettering, the Latin motto *Victoria Concordia Crescit* and the Islington coat of arms. ▶

This was the VCC crest, which was to remain virtually unchanged for the following 53 years.

For many years the crest appeared on players' shirts only for cup finals, although in the early finals it was more often not the cannon, but various other famous Arsenal emblems, such as the intertwined AFC monogram, that adorned the kit. This was supplanted by the single cannon motif for the FA Cup Final in the 1971 Double-winning year.

The crest had begun to appear on shirts for 'ordinary' matches four years earlier, at the start of the 1967/68 season. Initially, the single cannon motif was used; then, in 1990, the crest was incorporated into the home kit design, appearing on the away kit a year later.

In 2002, the Club replaced the gothic-style *Victoria Concordia Crescit* crest with a simpler, more stylised version of the cannon crest, under the ethos 'Tradition With Vision'. The cannon, as it had done in 1922, once again reverted to the east, as it had been from 1922 onwards.

See also: Victoria Concordia Crescit (page 111)

OTHER ARSENALS (4)

Arsenal Tula (Russia)
Distance from Highbury: 1,543 miles

Hailing from a provincial city 300 miles south of Moscow, Arsenal Tula owe their name, like their London namesakes, to an association with the munitions industry. Tula is most famous for producing the tanks that kept Hitler at bay during World War Two.

For half a century, its football team languished in the third flight. Then in 1996, head coach Yevgeny Kucherevsky went on a scouting mission to Brazil, returning with three players, the first Latin Americans to play in Russia. By the following season, Arsenal Tula had nine Brazilians on their books, and that set a trend for other Russian clubs, so that in 2003 there were more than 40 South Americans in the Russian Premier League.

In 1997, helped by their Brazilians, Arsenal Tula gained promotion to the Russian first division for the first time, and since then they have come close to reaching the premier flight.

ARSENAL RAF XI V THE RAF

During World War Two, Arsenal arranged a unique fixture to field an entire team of outfield players who were serving in the Royal Air Force – and the opposition was another RAF team!

Had it not been for an injury to another Arsenal RAF man, goalkeeper George Marks, they would have fielded a complete Gunners XI. Still, the stand-in keeper, Frank Boulton, was a former Arsenal player who had moved to Derby County just before the war.

Arsenal's selected line-up that day: Frank Boulton, Laurie Scott, Eddie Hapgood, Jack Crayston, Bernard Joy, George Male, Alf Kirchen, George Drury, Ted Drake, George Curtis, Leslie Jones.

The match, which like all of Arsenal's wartime 'home' games was played at White Hart Lane, ended in a 1–1 draw.

See also: Hapgood gets an armed escort to Spurs (page 138)

CHAPMAN INNOVATIONS (7)

Hoops

Arsenal have played in hooped socks at various stages in their history. They were yet another Herbert Chapman brainchild. As with the white-sleeved shirts, they were designed to help the players spot each other more easily on the pitch, and many other teams later followed suit.

On 4 March 1933, the day Arsenal's red-and-white kit was christened, they wore red-and-white hooped socks. Soon these were replaced by blue-and-white, which remained the colours of Arsenal socks until 1960, since when a plainer pattern has been used (generally a single colour with a one-band design).

On later occasions, Arsenal have reverted to the retro look, playing again in red-and-white hoops during the 1994/95 and 1995/96 seasons, in blue-and-white hoops in 1967/68 and 1968/69 and even red-and-black hoops in 1982/83.

2003 FA CUP FINAL

17 May 2003 • Millennium Stadium • Attendance: 73,726
Arsenal 1 Southampton 0 (Goal: Pires)
Formation: 4-4-2

SEAMAN

LAUREN

KEOWN

LUZHNY

COLE

LJUNGBERG

GILBERTO

PARLOUR

PIRES

BERGKAMP

HENRY

Sub used: 11 Wiltord (for Bergkamp)

HOBBIES OF THE 1913 ARSENAL SQUAD

Lievesley	Shooting	Greenaway	Lawn tennis
Benson	Motorcycling	Caldwell	Badminton
Shaw	Mountaineering	Groves	Whippet racing
Jobey	Reading	Randall	Sprinting
Sands	Oratory	Fidler	Aviation
Graham	Mathematics	McEachrane	Chess
Rutherford	Boxing	Thomson	Archery
Flanagan	Continental touring	Ford, G	Golf
Stonley	Croquet	Ford, W	Fencing
Hardinge	Ping-pong	Burrell	Big game shooting
Lewis	Yachting	King	Tobogganing
McKinnon	Foreign languages	Watson	Singing
Grant	Skating	Peart	Curling
Winship	Wrestling	Devine	Fives
Bell	Polo	Adams	Bowls

The manager, **George Morrell,** had a passion for hunting, while the Club's trainer, **George Hardy,** was a big clay-pigeon shooting fan.

SCREEN SHOTS

Ever since *The Arsenal Stadium Mystery* in 1939, the Gunners have featured regularly on the silver screen, but the references haven't always been quite so obvious. Here is a selection of cinematic nods to the Club that have appeared over the years.

The Baby Juice Express (2001)
Co-written by Arsenal fan Nick Moran, the film features the acting debuts of David Seaman (as Huge Gangster) and Ray Parlour (as Vince).

Corrupt (1983)
Former Sex Pistol John Lydon, a fan of the Gunners, co-stars with Harvey Keitel. During the film Lydon is shown carrying an Arsenal bag.

Coyote Ugly (2000)
The film features a scene in a music shop, where Joe Strummer's musical tribute to Tony Adams is playing loudly in the background.

Fever Pitch (1997)
Colin Firth stars in the film adaptation of Nick Hornby's famous novel of the same name, a chronicle of the joys and despair of a Gunners fan.

Frenzy (1972)
In this Hitchcock film, the pub where the hero works has a stained-glass window that pays tribute to Arsenal's Double-winning campaign of 1971.

The Full Monty (1997)
In one scene the group are trying to master their routine and do so after one of them explains it as the Arsenal back four playing the offside trap.

Lamb (1985)
Liam Neeson plays a priest who runs away from Dublin to London with a young epileptic boy to help him fulfil his dreams, including a trip to Arsenal. They are shown on the North Bank. David O'Leary is mentioned.

Muggers (2000)
This film was produced by a company called Clock End Films and the Gunners-supporting producer makes a brief appearance as an extra, sporting an Arsenal scarf. In the closing credits, Arsenal FC are thanked for winning the Double in 1998 and 'for being an abiding inspiration.'

Ocean's 12 (2004)
George Clooney and Brad Pitt wear Arsenal tracksuits to help them escape during a complex scam in a variety of European cities.

Plunkett And Macleane (1999)
Robert Carlyle and Jonny Lee Miller are 18th-century London highwaymen. Lord Dorchester has two henchmen called Dixon and Winterburn.

When Saturday Comes (1996)
At one point during this film, which follows Sean Bean's quest to star for Sheffield United, the Blades play Arsenal. Bean is on the bench.

The Young Americans (1993)
A US gangster movie, starring Harvey Keitel again, which features a scene at Highbury with footage of a real match.

See also: The Arsenal Stadium Mystery (page 124) and Strummer on Adams (page 84)

CHAMPION GUNNERS (12)

Premiership 2001/02

	P	Home					Away					Pt
		W	D	L	F	A	W	D	L	F	A	
Arsenal	38	12	4	3	42	25	14	5	0	37	11	87
Liverpool	38	12	5	2	33	14	12	3	4	34	16	80
Manchester Utd	38	11	2	6	40	17	13	3	3	47	28	77
Newcastle Utd	38	12	3	4	40	23	9	5	5	34	29	71
Leeds Utd	38	9	6	4	31	21	9	6	4	22	16	66
Chelsea	38	11	4	4	43	21	6	9	4	23	17	64
West Ham Utd	38	12	4	3	32	14	3	4	12	16	43	53
Aston Villa	38	8	7	4	22	17	4	7	8	24	30	50
Tottenham H	38	10	4	5	32	24	4	4	11	17	29	50
Blackburn R	38	8	6	5	33	20	4	4	11	22	31	46
Southampton	38	7	5	7	23	22	5	4	10	23	32	45
Middlesbrough	38	7	5	7	23	26	5	4	10	12	21	45
Fulham	38	7	7	5	21	16	3	7	9	15	28	44
Charlton Ath	38	5	6	8	23	30	5	8	6	15	19	44
Everton	38	8	4	7	26	23	3	6	10	19	34	43
Bolton W	38	5	7	7	20	31	4	6	9	24	31	40
Sunderland	38	7	7	5	18	16	3	3	13	11	35	40
Ipswich Town	38	6	4	9	20	24	3	5	11	21	40	36
Derby County	38	5	4	10	20	26	3	2	14	13	37	30
Leicester City	38	3	7	9	15	34	2	6	11	15	30	28

TRENDSETTERS

- Thierry Henry's socks-at-full-mast style is a silent tribute to one of his footballing heroes, Brazilian striker Sonny Anderson, who was at Monaco when Henry was a youngster with the club and who wears his socks the same way.

- Alex James was renowned for wearing his shorts extra-long, hence his nickname 'Old Baggy Shorts'. He got the idea when he saw a caricature of himself by *Daily Mail* cartoonist Tom Webster, who had depicted him wearing shorts down to his knees. James was tickled by the image, and went out and ordered himself some voluminous shorts, which soon became his trademark.

- In the 1970s Alan Ball was known for playing in white boots, decades before they became a more commonplace fashion statement on the football field.

- Almost seven decades before Ball, Herbert Chapman showed early signs of being a football pioneer, when as a player with Spurs he took to the field wearing yellow boots!

GROUND'S-EYE VIEW

A matchday in the life of current Arsenal head groundsman, Paul Burgess:

'I'll be awake at 5.30 am and make sure that I'm down at the stadium an hour later to meet with my assistant, Paul Ashcroft. Our first task is to get straight out on to the pitch to brush the morning dew from the surface, which takes about half an hour.

At 7 am we'll cut the pitch width-ways. The grass is cut to approximately an inch high, though in hot weather we cut it to three-quarters of an inch to allow for additional growth on the day. This takes about two hours. Then we repeat the exercise length-ways to create the criss-cross pattern. The stripes on the pitch are mainly for presentation, but they also serve to help the linesmen in making offside decisions.

At 11 am we'll turn the sprinklers on and give the pitch a brief watering before we mark the lines, which we do fresh for every game. At 1 pm we'll put out the temporary goals for the goalkeepers' warm-up. This helps to ensure that the actual goalmouths are protected as much as possible.

At 2 pm, I'll walk the pitch to make sure that it's spotless. Sometimes the referee will chat to me before the game about the weather conditions, or perhaps the timing of when the floodlights should go on. At half-time, myself, Paul and seven 'divoters' who work with us on matchdays will repair any damage to the pitch.

Then at full-time we are back on the pitch with our forks for about an hour. We usually leave the ground at about 11pm, although we have been known to finish as late as 3 am! As long as the players are happy, it is worthwhile.'

DOUBLE INTERNATIONALS

Four Gunners have represented England at football and cricket. They were **Wally Hardinge, Andy Ducat, Denis Compton** and **Arthur Milton**.

MORE ARSENAL CRICKETING FACTS

- During his time at the Club, Herbert Chapman actively encouraged the cricketing pursuits of his players during the summer. Not only did it provide them with a means of keeping fit during the lay-off, it also ensured that the name of Arsenal remained in the spotlight even when there was no football.

- Wally Hardinge scored more than 35,000 runs for Kent.

- During the 1950/51 season, the Club had no fewer than five county cricketers on their books (Leslie Compton, Don Roper, Jimmy Gray, Brian Close and Arthur Milton), with another player (Cliff Holton), who represented Oxfordshire in the Minor Counties championship.

- Arthur Milton won one football cap for England in 1951, making him the last double international.

- Brian Close set three major cricketing records: he became the youngest cricketer to play for England, the youngest to represent the Yorkshire first team, and also the youngest all-rounder to take 100 wickets and score 1,000 runs in a single season. He also played more than 40 Tests for England.

- Samuel Hill-Wood, former director and chairman of Arsenal, and grandfather of current incumbent Peter Hill-Wood, opened the batting for Derbyshire and once scored ten runs off one ball against the MCC.

- Arsenal defender Steve Gatting, brother of the former England cricket captain Mike, played cricket for the Middlesex second XI.

THE LOST CAPTAIN

A poetic tribute to Herbert Chapman, penned shortly after his death in 1934 by his assistant, Joe Shaw:

> The Last Whistle has sounded, the great game is over,
> O was ever a field left so silent as this;
> The scene a bright hour since, how empty it is;
> What desolate splendour the shadows now cover.
> The captain has gone. The splendour was his.
>
> He made no farewell, no sign has he given
> That for him nevermore shall the big ball roll,
> Nor the players he urged on, from his strong heart and soul,
> Strive again with his skill, as they always have striven.
> Not again will he hear when the crowd shouts: 'Goal!'
>
> But somewhere . . . somewhere his spirit will quicken
> With victors and vanquished. For now he has cast
> In his lot with the Olympians of old who outlast
> This human encounter, this football so stricken
> That it seemed for a moment to die when he passed.
>
> Who shall challenge his name, who shall challenge the laurel
> We hold out to him through the twilight? His love
> Was in beauty of action, and clean limbs that move
> With the pride of high combat above the mean quarrel.
> He led others to share it. And that is enough.
>
> Not yet for those others the Full-Time is blowing.
> The ball will roll on, they will cheer with their throats aflame;
> They will think how this steel-minded man in his fame
> Had dreamed while he worked, a dream ever glowing,
> Of the glory of Greece in an English game.

— HAPGOOD GETS AN ARMED ESCORT TO SPURS —

One Saturday morning, early in his time with the RAF at the start of World War Two, Eddie Hapgood found himself confined to barracks for failing to stand to attention while addressing an officer (a charge that was later dismissed). That same day he was due to captain Arsenal in a north London derby at White Hart Lane.

After much persuasion, he managed to convince the duty sergeant to allow him a few hours leave for the afternoon so that he could play in the match, but only on the condition that he was accompanied by an armed escort!

He had to travel to the ground in a military vehicle, in the company of two warrant officers, who duly escorted him into the dressing room and even insisted on flanking him as he led the team on to the pitch.

See also: Arsenal RAF XI v the RAF (page 130)

—————— FIRST WAS THE WORD ——————

The word 'arsenal' is derived from the Arabic *dar-as-sina*, meaning 'house of industry' or 'house of skill'. In the 15th century it appeared in Spanish and Italian as *darsena*, meaning 'dock'. However, the Venetians adopted a slightly different form – *arsenale*. To this day the naval dockyard in Venice is called the Arzenale.

In *A History of Italy*, published in 1549, William Thomas wrote of the Venice dockyard:

> *'The Arsenale in myne eye excedeth all the rest: For there they haue well neere two hundred galeys.'*

Roughly translated, what he was saying was: 'In my eyes the Arsenale is greater than all the others; they have almost two hundred galleys there.'

In 16th-century English, 'arsenal' came to mean a naval warehouse; and later still, it was used to refer more generally to any sort of military stores or armaments factory – such as the Royal Arsenal at Woolwich.

THE LEAGUE DEBUT

On 2 September 1893 Woolwich Arsenal played their first League fixture, at home to Newcastle United in the Second Division. It was a momentous occasion, rendered all the more so because, for the first two seasons after turning professional, they had been banned from all previous cup competitions apart from the FA Cup.

It took Arsenal just six minutes to open their League account, when Shaw fired into the net to huge cheers from the crowd. They then defended their lead well and at half time it was 1–0 to the Arsenal!

Early in the second period the advantage was doubled when Elliott got on the end of a pass from Booth. Unfortunately Arsenal were unable to resist a determined United side who eventually got back into the match to claim an honourable draw.

Woolwich Arsenal · Formation: 2-3-5

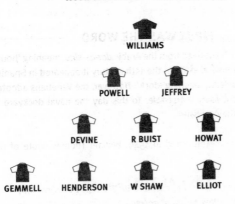

THE THINGS THEY SAY (9)

'Fighting qualities and team spirit are the most essential features of an Arsenal team. Opponents know them as the men who never give in. Whatever the odds they refuse to accept defeat until the final whistle sounds.'

Bernard Joy, Arsenal centre half (1935–46), in Forward Arsenal.

OLDEST AND YOUNGEST

Outside right Jock Rutherford was 41 years and 159 days old when he took his final bow for Arsenal in the home match against Manchester City on 20 March 1926. Rutherford had joined from Newcastle United 13 years earlier during the Club's first season at Highbury.

Spanish midfielder Francesc 'Cesc' Fabregas made his first-team debut at home to Rotherham United in the Carling Cup on 28 October 2003, aged 16 years and 177 days. In the next round, against Wolves – aged 16 years and 212 days – he scored his first goal for Arsenal, thus replacing Stewart Robson as the Club's youngest scorer in a competitive match.

ROYAL ORDNANCE

When Arsenal turned professional in 1891, the workers at Woolwich Arsenal soon decided they wanted to maintain an amateur team, and so a new outfit called Royal Ordnance Factories FC was formed. Five ex-Arsenal players featured in their early line-ups, and they played their home matches at the Invicta Ground, previously occupied by Arsenal.

On 25 April 1895, after Royal Ordnance moved to a new ground, they organised a fixture against Woolwich Arsenal to christen it. Despite the obvious gulf in class between the amateurs and pros – Arsenal put out a near full-strength side – Royal Ordnance managed to pull off a remarkable 1–0 victory.

CAPITAL TITLE GAINS

Arsenal have clinched eight of their 13 League titles in London, but only four of them at Highbury (in 1931, 1938, 1953 and 1998). The Gunners have twice been confirmed as champions at both White Hart Lane (1971 and 2004) and at Stamford Bridge (1933 and 1934).

The other 'title-winning' grounds were Ayresome Park (1935), Leeds Road (1948), Anfield (1989) and Old Trafford (2002). In 1991, Arsenal were confirmed as champions on a day when they weren't playing, thanks to results elsewhere.

HAT-TRICK HEROES

Arsenal's leading hat-trick scorers:

Ted Drake	12*
Jack Lambert	12
Jimmy Brain	12
Ian Wright	11
Doug Lishman	8
Thierry Henry	7
David Herd	7
David Jack	7
John Radford	6
Joe Baker	5
Ronnie Rooke	5
Joe Baker	5

Ninety different players have scored a total of 210* hat-tricks for Arsenal in competitive fixtures since 1889, when the Club first entered the FA Cup. Two players, Barbour and Scott, hold the honour as Woolwich Arsenal's first hat-trick scorers, both netting three times in an FA Cup victory over Lyndhurst on 5 October 1889.

Includes one double hat-trick

CROSS-PARTY SUPPORT

Arsenal enjoy considerable cross-party support in both the House of Commons and the House of Lords. Here are a few politicos known to have red (and white) leanings:

Iain Coleman MP (Conservative)
Jeremy Corbyn MP (Labour)
Chris Smith MP (Labour)
Lord Winston (Labour)
Lord Harris (Conservative)
Lord Marshall (cross-bench)
Lord Preston (Labour)
Lord Simon (Labour)
Lord Clinton-Davies (Labour)

NUMBER CRUNCHING (11)

44: the number of goals scored in all competitions by Ted Drake for Arsenal in the 1934/35 season – a Club record. Of those, 42 came in the League, which is another Club record.

DERBY DAZZLER (8)

THIERRY HENRY
16 November 2002 • Arsenal 3 Spurs 0
Premiership, Highbury

Henry collects the ball from a throw-in inside the Arsenal half and embarks on a run, outpacing first Etherington, then Richards and King, before unleashing a low drive from 20 yards into the corner of the net in front of a jubilant North Bank – one of the finest solo goals ever at Highbury, and that it comes against Spurs makes it even more special.

THE LAST OF THE ENGLISH ELEVENS

The last time Arsenal fielded a starting XI in the League made up entirely of English players was on 19 April 1994, when George Graham named the following team, in 4-3-3 formation, for a home match against Wimbledon:

Sub: 12 Flatts (also English)

The match ended 1–1, with Steve Bould scoring for Arsenal. The very last time Arsenal started with an all-English XI was in the Coca-Cola Cup at Hartlepool United on 21 September 1994 when the team was as above, with Linighan for Bould and Merson for Campbell. Arsenal have never fielded a starting team consisting entirely of overseas players. Ten non-English players were fielded a few times in the 2003/04 season, the last of which was 16 April, when the team against Leeds United was:

Subs used: 17 Edu (for Gilberto), 15 Parlour (for Pires), 9 Reyes (for Bergkamp)

PITCH RESCUE

One morning in 1996, staff at Highbury were rather taken aback to see a helicopter make an impromptu landing on the middle of the pitch. 'We were having a meeting in one of the executive boxes,' recalls Director Ken Friar, 'when there was a huge noise, and literally out of the blue a helicopter descended onto the pitch in front of us like some sort of yellow spaceship.' The helicopter, the London Air Ambulance, had been called in after a construction worker on a nearby building site had been the victim of a massive electric shock, and the Arsenal pitch was the only place it could land. Within moments the pitch was overrun with paramedics, and an ambulance, entering through the South Stand gate, arrived with the victim, who was then airlifted to hospital.

NAMING THE NEW HOME

When Arsenal moved from Woolwich to Highbury in 1913, the question of the new stadium's name became the subject of discussion, within the Club and among its supporters. Here are a few of the suggestions:

Avesbury Park: from Mr W Dykes of Camden Town, who thought that a combination of Avenell Road and Highbury would be a fitting name.

The Fortress: from Mr HW Cooper of Islington. As he wrote: 'We hear of the Canary and his Nest at Norwich, and the Lion in his Den at Millwall, so why not the Gunner in his Fortress?'

The Gun Park: from 'Iddy', as a further nod to the Club's origins.

Mr Cooper did not see his preference adopted, but he can claim success with one of his other suggestions. The Arsenal programme editor noted: 'An idea suggested by Mr Cooper for indicating goalscorers is quite good. When the time is ripe we may try it.'

1994 EUROPEAN CUP WINNERS' CUP FINAL

4 May 1994 • Parken Stadium, Copenhagen • Attendance: 33,765
Arsenal 1 Parma 0 (Goal: Smith)
Formation: 4-4-2

SEAMAN

DIXON

BOULD

ADAMS

WINTERBURN

DAVIS

SELLEY

MORROW

MERSON

CAMPBELL

SMITH

Sub used: 14 McGoldrick (for Merson)

THE MAN WHO STARTED IT ALL

One man who, more than any other, was responsible for bringing Arsenal into existence was David Danskin, a Scot of Polish descent, who hailed from Burntisland in Fife. He was the first of many Scots who would play a key role in Arsenal over the next century.

Danskin moved to London in 1885, at the age of 22, in search of work after completing his apprenticeship as an engine fitter. Soon he found a job at the Woolwich Arsenal, in the Dial Square gun workshop.

Like many Scots he was a keen footballer, and had earned his stripes as captain of Kirkcaldy Wanderers. Dial Square already had a cricket team, and soon he persuaded some of his new colleagues that they should have a football team, too.

Danskin put a subscription list together, collecting sixpence (equivalent to two-and-a-half pence) from each of 15 colleagues, and contributing extra from his own pocket to make it up to ten shillings and sixpence (52½ pence) – enough to purchase a football.

So it was that Dial Square FC was born in October 1886. Danskin, who became the team's first captain, played regularly until 1889, when injury forced him to limit his appearances, but he did take the role of stand-in goalkeeper a couple of seasons later.

See also: Pitch imperfect (page 85)

THIERRY HENRY

Sung to the tune of *Tom Hark*

Went down the Lane, the other night
To tell the Spurs we got the new Ian Wright
They said to me: 'How can that be?'
I said to them: 'We've got Thierry Henry'
Thierry Henry, Thierry Henry,
Thierry Henry, (we got) Thierry Henry.

Premiership 2003/04

	P		Home					Away				Pt
		W	D	L	F	A	W	D	L	F	A	
Arsenal	**38**	**15**	**4**	**0**	**40**	**14**	**11**	**8**	**0**	**33**	**12**	**90**
Chelsea	38	12	4	3	34	13	12	3	4	33	17	79
Manchester Utd	38	12	4	3	37	15	11	2	6	27	20	75
Liverpool	38	10	4	5	29	15	6	8	5	26	22	60
Newcastle Utd	38	11	5	3	33	14	2	12	5	19	26	56
Aston Villa	38	9	6	4	24	19	6	5	8	24	25	56
Charlton Ath	38	7	6	6	29	29	7	5	7	22	22	53
Bolton W	38	6	8	5	24	21	8	3	8	24	35	53
Fulham	38	9	4	6	29	21	5	6	8	23	25	52
Birmingham C	38	8	5	6	26	24	4	9	6	17	24	50
Middlesbrough	38	8	4	7	25	23	5	5	9	19	29	48
Southampton	38	8	6	5	24	17	4	5	10	20	28	47
Portsmouth	38	10	4	5	35	19	2	5	12	12	35	45
Tottenham H	38	9	4	6	33	27	4	2	13	14	30	45
Blackburn R	38	5	4	10	25	31	7	4	8	26	28	44
Manchester C	38	5	9	5	31	24	4	5	10	24	30	41
Everton	38	8	5	6	27	20	1	7	11	18	37	39
Leicester City	38	3	10	6	19	28	3	5	11	29	37	33
Leeds Utd	38	5	7	7	25	31	3	2	14	15	48	33
Wolves	38	7	5	7	23	35	0	7	12	15	42	33

—————— **HERBERT CHAPMAN'S PLAYING CAREER** ——————

Before venturing into management at the tender age of 29, Herbert Chapman played for a host of clubs as an inside forward.

As an amateur between 1897 and 1901 he served:

Kiveton Park
Ashton North End
Stalybridge Rovers
Rochdale
Grimsby Town
Swindon Town
Sheppey United
Worksop

As a professional shortly after the turn of the century the great man wore the colours of:

Northampton Town (1901–02)
Sheffield United (1902–03)
Notts County (1903–04)
Northampton Town [again] (1904)
Tottenham Hotspur (1905–07)

See also: Chapman's managerial spurs (page 37)

Dr Highbury made regular appearances in the Arsenal programme for several seasons after the Club moved to north London in 1913. He made his debut on 6 September 1913, here seen providing the Club with a clean bill of health after a life-saving move north of the River Thames.

Arsenal welcomes fans to Highbury, for the first match at the new stadium versus Leicester Fosse on 6 September 1913.

THE FIRST MATCH AT HIGHBURY

Arsenal played their first match at Highbury on 6 September 1913, against Leicester Fosse (the old name of Leicester City). It was a winning start, the game ending in a 2–1 victory to the Gunners. Interestingly, Arsenal did not drop Woolwich from their name after their move north of the River Thames until towards the end of the 1913/14 season. That historic day's team, in 2-3-5 formation, was:

KEN FRIAR'S ARSENAL TIMELINE

1946 – Aged 11, begins working for Arsenal as an errand boy

1950 – Employed by the Club as an office junior in the box office

1954 – Moves to the Club's accounts department

1965 – Appointed Assistant Club Secretary

1972 – Appointed Club Secretary

1983 – Named as Managing Director and appointed to the board

2000 – Awarded OBE in the Queen's Birthday Honours List. Retires as MD, but stays on to head up Arsenal's relocation to Ashburton Grove, together with Danny Fiszman.

GREAT SCOTS

Arsenal's Scottish connections extend right back to day one of the Club's existence, when David Danskin of Kirkcaldy founded Dial Square FC in 1886. Since then more than 160 Scots have played for the Gunners.

From the wizardry of Alex James in the 1930s and Jimmy Logie in the 1950s, to Frank McLintock's captaining of the first Double-winning side of 1971 and the trophy-lifting spree under George Graham in the 1980s and 1990s, Scots have played a key role in the Club's most glorious chapters.

Ten notable Arsenal Scots through the decades:

James Charteris (1888–90)

Gavin Crawford (1891–98)

Billy Blyth (1914–29)

Frank Hill (1932–36)

Alex James (1929–37)

Jimmy Logie (1939–55)

Alex Forbes (1948–56)

George Graham (1966–72)

Frank McLintock (1964–73)

Charlie Nicholas (1983–88)

Aside from **George Graham** (1986–95), Arsenal have had four other Scottish managers:

Thomas Brown Mitchell (1897–98)

Phil Kelso (1904–1908)

George Morrell (1908–1915) ▸

Bruce Rioch (1995–1996, although born in Aldershot, he qualified to play for Scotland through his parents)

At least five Scots captained Arsenal prior to **Frank McLintock,** including:

David Danskin

Gavin Crawford

James Jackson

Billy Blyth

Alex James

THE MARGATE NURSERY

For four seasons before World War Two, from 1934/35 to 1937/38, Margate FC were Arsenal's nursery team. The idea was that of George Allison, whose daughter went to school in nearby Thanet. 'In the past we have suffered very much because we have been unable to take likely boys of 18 or 19 found by our scouts,' Arsenal Chairman Sir Samuel Hill-Wood told the *Thanet Gazette*, explaining the reasoning behind the idea. 'What we wanted was some club willing and good enough to teach our young players for us. We can and do find lots of promising young boys but they must have somewhere to play and be taught.'

Under the arrangement, Arsenal paid 60 per cent of the Margate players' wages, and appointed their own manager, ex-player James Ramsay, with former Spurs manager Peter McWilliam as scout. They also helped to revamp the Kent club's stadium. Arsenal had recently completed their new East Stand, and seats from the old stand were used to rebuild Margate's North Stand. Meanwhile, the Margate pitch was re-laid to match the dimensions at Highbury. Future Welsh international Horace Cumner, George Marks, Alf Fields and Reg Lewis were among half a dozen or so Margate youngsters who made it into the Arsenal senior team; and many others ended up with other top flight teams. Margate also benefited from occasional appearances by seasoned Arsenal pros such as goalkeeper Charlie Preedy, and centre forward Jack Lambert, who later took over as manager of the nursery club.

FAR-FLUNG FANS

Official Arsenal Supporters Clubs

Iceland Arsenal Supporters Club
Founded: 1983
Contact: Jóhann Freyr Ragnarsson
Email: joiragg@isholf.is
Website: www.arsenal.is
Fact: Almost 1 per cent of the population of Iceland are members of the Arsenal Supporters Club

Denmark Arsenal Football Supporters Club
Founded: 1991
Contact: Thomas Ballegaard
Email: tb@arsenal.dk
Website: www.arsenal.dk
Fact: Tony Adams is president of the supporters club, while honorary members include John Jensen and Jan Molby

Norway Arsenal Supporters Club
Founded: 1979
Contact: Petter Randmæl
Email: kontakt@gunners.no
Website: www.gunners.no
Fact: The supporters club's honorary president is Frank McLintock

Sweden Arsenal Supporters Club
Founded: 2001
Contact: Mats Willner
Email: mats.willner@nt.se
Website: www.arsenal.se
Fact: A favourite meeting place for supporters club members is the Limp Bar in Stockholm, run by former Arsenal favourite, Anders Limpar

South Africa Arsenal Supporters Club
Founded: 1991
Contact: David Honey
Email: honeyd@telkomsa.net
Fact: Former Gunners Alex Forbes and George Eastham, who now live in South Africa, are both honorary members of the supporters club

Australian Arsenal Supporters Club
Founded: 1987
Contact: Micky Brock
Email: dbrock@vtown.com.au
Fact: A group of AASC members are hoping to make a 10,000-mile-plus pilgrimage to London to attend the opening game at the new Ashburton stadium in 2006

Arsenal America
Founded: 2001
Contact: Rick Liebling
Email: rick@arsenalamerica.com
Website: www.arsenalamerica.com
Fact: Over 50 per cent of hits on the Official Arsenal Website in 2003 were registered in the USA

Japanese Arsenal Supporters Club
Founded: 2001
Contact: Mika Campbell
Email: mika@blueyonder.co.uk
Fact: Kura-San, who claims to be Arsenal's oldest fan in Japan, first watched them play as a teenager, when they toured Japan in 1967

Cyprus Arsenal Supporters Club
Founded: 1992
Contact: Vasos Christoforou
Email: stevens.rental@cytanet.com.cy
Fact: In December 2002, Arsenal took the Championship trophy and the FA Cup to Cyprus and displayed them to a gathering of over 700 local Arsenal fans

Italy Arsenal Supporters Club
Founded: 2000
Contact: Luca Frazzi
Email: lucafrazzi@libero.it
Website: www.arsenalfansclub.4t.com
Fact: In 2003, Luca Frazzi penned *Lontano da Highbury* (A long way from Highbury), the first book about Arsenal written in Italian

IT'S UP FOR GRABS NOW!

'And Arsenal come streaming forward in what will surely be their last attack. A good ball by Dixon, finding Smith, to Thomas, charging through the midfield. It's up for grabs now!'

From Brian Moore's commentary on Liverpool v Arsenal, late spring 1989

Division One · 26 May 1989 · Anfield · Attendance: 41,718
Liverpool 0 Arsenal 2 (Goals: Smith, Thomas)
Formation: 5-4-1

LUKIC

DIXON   ADAMS   O'LEARY   BOULD   WINTERBURN

ROCASTLE   RICHARDSON   THOMAS   MERSON

SMITH

Subs used: 14 Hayes (for Merson), 12 Groves (for Bould)

It was probably the most dramatic climax to a season ever witnessed – in England, or anywhere else. Arsenal needed a win by two goals or more to pip opponents and reigning champions Liverpool to the title on their own turf. A 1–0 second-half lead courtesy of Alan Smith's header wasn't going to be enough. Then, with 91 minutes and 27 seconds on the clock, up popped Michael Thomas to net one of the most famous Arsenal goals of all time and take the crown to Highbury on goals scored.

	P	W	D	L	F	A	GD	Pts
Arsenal	38	22	10	6	73	36	37	76
Liverpool	38	22	10	6	65	28	37	76

Season Tickets

are now ready, and one is at your disposal in exchange for 21s , entitling you to admission to ground —Avenell Road entrance— and a Seat in the Grand Stand for all the Club Matches during the Season (Cup Ties excepted). This is a very low price, especially having regard to the large number of matches to be played (See Fixtures List on inside of back cover). Lady's or Boy's Tickets are 15s. each. All Tickets are transferable, and a special discount is allowed to Shareholders. The Secretary's name is GEO. MORRELL. His address is 32, Pemberton Road, Harringay. . . . He wants to sell you a ticket. Do not let him be disappointed.

* * *

Why not identify yourself with the Club by becoming a Shareholder ?

The Shares are £1 each and can, if desired, be paid for by 4 monthly payments.

You will not miss the small payment and will help to add to the general comfort and efficiency.

Not only that, but you can get your Season Ticket cheaper, with a special seat in a special part of the Stand.

The Secretary is Mr. Morrell. His address is 32, Pemberton Road, Harringay, and he is waiting to hear from you.

* * *

In 1913, those wishing to become Arsenal shareholders or season-ticket holders in the Club's first season in north London were invited to apply by writing to the home address of Secretary-Manager, George Morrell.

ARSÈNE WHO?

'Arsène who?' screamed many of the headlines when a new Arsenal manager took the helm in 1996. It didn't take them long to find out, and he has since become one of the men that the press love to quote. Here are a few memorable 'Wengerisms':

'You can never escape the history of a Club like this. At some clubs success is accidental, but at Arsenal it is compulsory.'
April 1998

'Everyone thinks they have the prettiest wife at home.'
Responding to comments by Sir Alex Ferguson on the relative merits of Manchester United and Arsenal, April 2002

'I can go home at night knowing this team will give every last drop of their blood for me and Arsenal.'
May 2002

'He also has incredible speed and power. He's the quickest player at Arsenal – he even beat me just by a fraction!'
On Thierry Henry, December 2003

'Sometimes it can just be a fight for 90 minutes, both teams give everything and you can enjoy it, but there must be something more as well. It's like the theatre. There is a magical moment in the second act and when you go home you remember that. It can happen with a football team as well.'
In The Glorious Game, Alex Flynn and Kevin Whitcher

'I'm very grateful for the honour and I'm grateful to England for creating the sport. I don't know what I would do without it.'
On receiving his OBE in June 2003

'Maybe there is someone in this world who can imitate my voice and has my chequebook as he buys players every day.'
Responding to transfer speculation linking Arsenal to French goalkeeper, Sebastian Frey, January 2004

*'We won't relax because of this. When it is going well,
be humble and rigorous. We have to show we are intelligent
people and be more demanding of ourselves.'*
Reflecting on Arsenal's history-making defeat of Blackburn Rovers,
which secured a new English record of 43 consecutive league
matches unbeaten. The Guardian, August 2004

*'The board are very supportive. It's a 100 per cent supportive
atmosphere and that's why I'm still here. There was a time when the
board had to be strong and they were. That's what makes the Club
special, as there's a trust that you don't find in many places.'*
April 2004

*'I might have gone into politics ... I like the idea of a profession
which you can do for your whole life. For example, I admire [the
pianist] Rubinstein, who at 83 was still able to perform concerts.
I hate the idea of retiring!'*
When asked what he might have done if he couldn't
have chosen football, Tonic Magazine, 2000

— PORTUGUNNERS —

The Portuguese first division side, Sporting Braga, have been known as
Arsenal do Minho or Arsenal do Braga ever since the club swapped their
green-and-white colours for a red-and-white strip, almost identical to that
of the Gunners, in the 1930s. The man behind the new kit was the club's
former coach, Jose Szabo, inspired after a visit to London, where he
watched the Gunners play. More recently the club actually had a youth
team which was officially called Arsenal do Braga.

2005 FA CUP FINAL

FA Cup Final • 18 May 2005 • Millennium Stadium • Attendance: 71,876
Arsenal 0 Manchester Utd 0 (aet)
Arsenal won 5–4 on penalties
Formation: 4-5-1

LEHMANN

LAUREN

TOURE

SENDEROS

COLE

PIRES

FABREGAS

VIEIRA

GILBERTO

REYES

BERGKAMP

Subs used: 8 Ljungberg (for Bergkamp), 11 Van Persie (for Fabregas), 17 Edu (for Pires)

SELECTED BIBLIOGRAPHY

Books

Bastin, Clifford, *Cliff Bastin remembers: An autobiography*, Etterick Press, London, 1950

Connolly, Kevin, *The Official Arsenal Factfile*, Hamlyn, London, 2002

Downing, David, *Passavotchka*, Bloomsbury, London, 2000

Fynn, Alex, and Whitcher, Kevin, *The Glorious Game: Arsene Wenger, Arsenal and the Quest for Success*, Orion, London, 2003

Hapgood, Eddie, *Football Ambassador*, Sporting Handbooks, London, 1945

Joy, Bernard, *Forward Arsenal*, Phoenix House, London, 1952

Ollier, Fred, *Arsenal: A Complete Record, 1886–1992*, Breedon Books, Derby, 1992

Palmer, Myles, *The Professor: Arsène Wenger at Arsenal*, Virgin, London, 2002

Pickering, David, *Cassell's Sporting Quotations*, Cassell, London, 2000

Rees, Jasper, *Wenger: The Making of a Legend*, Short Books, London, 2003

Roper, Alan, *The Real Arsenal Story – In the years of Gog*, Wherry Publishing, Norwich, 2004

Stuff, Stephen, *Herbert Chapman, Football Emperor: A Study in the Origins of Modern Soccer*, Souvenir Press, London, 1998

(NB: Originally published in hardback in 1981, by Peter Owen Ltd, London)

Tossell, David, *Seventy-One Guns: The Year of the First Arsenal Double*, Mainstream Publishing, Edinburgh 2003

Other sources

Arsenal Football Club Publications

Arsenal Football Club Matchday Programmes 1908–2004

The Official Arsenal Club Manual

The Official Arsenal Handbook

The Official Arsenal Magazine, Volumes 1 and 2, 2002–04

Main online sources

The Official Arsenal Website: http://www.arsenal.com

Steve Gleiber's Arsenal Page: http://www.fl.net.au/~steve/index.htm

Arseweb: http://www.arseweb.com

The Jack Kelsey Fan Club: http://www.arsenalarsenal.co.uk

ACKNOWLEDGEMENTS

Author acknowledgements
With special thanks to Arsenal's publications team of Andy Exley,
Josh James and Svein Clouston for being a constant source of suggestions
and ideas. And to Ken Friar, for being so generous with his time when he
had more important matters on his mind.

Thanks are due also to Ivan Ponting, Alf Fields, Arthur Shaw, John
Jensen, John Devine, Alan Sunderland, Peter Marinello, Charlie George,
George Wood, Brian Hornsby, David Price, Stuart MacFarlane, Dan
Tolhurst, Katie Willis, Kate Lewis, Richard Clarke, Paul Burgess, Jill
Smith, Brian Glanville, Iain Cooke, Joe Cohen, David Duncan, Luca Frazzi,
Thomas Ballegaard, Kjartan Bjarnsson, Ingi Albertsson, Jói Ragg, Vasos
Christoforou, Micky Brock, Glen Bennett, Mats Wilner, Rick Liebling,
Mika Campbell, Steve Gleiber, Erling Kagge, Stephen Constantine.

Publisher acknowledgements
The Publisher would like to thank Betty Gardland for kindly allowing
us to use the work of Swedish artist Jan-Erik Garland (1905–1988).

Extract of *Filth* by Irvine Welsh published by Jonathan Cape.
Used by permission of The Random House Group Limited.

Consultant Editor **Fred Ollier**

Executive Editor **Trevor Davies**
Project Editor **Jessica Cowie**
Executive Art Editor **Jo MacGregor**
Design **'ome design**
Production Manager **Ian Paton**